When to Talk and When to Fight

The Strategic Choice between Dialogue and Resistance

Rebecca Subar

Graphics by Rosi Greenberg

ISBN: 978–1–62963–836–2 (print)
ISBN: 978–1–62963–852–2 (ebook)
Library of Congress Control Number: 2020934729

Cover by John Yates / www.stealworks.com
Cover illustration by Rosi Greenberg
Interior design by briandesign

10 9 8 7 6 5 4 3 2 1

PM Press
PO Box 23912
Oakland, CA 94623
www.pmpress.org

Printed in the USA.

Contents

SECTION III
Just and Sound Strategy in Practice

To Nava and Yonah

To everything there is a time, and for every pursuit a season
A time to throw stones and a time to gather stones
A time of war and a time of peace
—Ecclesiastes

I swear it's not too late
—Pete Seeger

Foreword

Esteban Kelly

Life in the United States is starkly unjust. We fight our way through an economy still fueled by the aftershocks of chattel slavery run atop a massive land grab from Indigenous people. Like Rebecca, I work with communities that have a clear vision of how life here can be different. Many have been fighting back and fighting to advance that vision for generations. The groups Rebecca and I tend to guide mobilize people to build power in pursuit of such change. Rebecca calls these communities of fighters.

Typically, when I facilitate an internal strategy session or an anti-racism training for a group of "fighters"—folks I usually refer to as organizers—we don't do much fighting at all. We take pains to build virtual containers designed to hold hard work. We take the folks assembled in the room and focus on solidarity with workers and exploited groups building power in their communities and across the world. When they're effective, groups gathered to fight for power spend most of their time and energy building relationships, nurturing liberatory communities, healing from persistent trauma, strategizing together, devising plans, solving problems, and sorting out our internal struggles. In short, we listen, we think, and we talk. We have that versatility of skills woven deep within our culture.

Still, I think many of us aren't as practiced at parsing the choice that Rebecca elevates in this book. Our communities need this toolkit—in many ways, that's what this book offers—because we'll benefit from more clarity, agility, and discernment to sort out when to go to the mat versus when to talk, negotiate, or even appease. We practice our fighting regimen so often it becomes second nature. Seasoned organizers have hindsight awareness of times our struggles might have advanced through talk, when instead we fought.

I recall the dizzying confusion I experienced back in 2005 when I felt responsible for navigating this "fight or talk" dilemma on a vast scale. I was young but not inexperienced around tensions within so-called mission-driven organizations. At the age of twenty-four, I was director of education and training for NASCO, a binational (Canada and the US) association of students and activists owning and managing cooperatives, primarily as affordable, autonomous, off-campus housing.[1] Their grassroots membership is extraordinarily diverse: white English-speaking middle-class kids comingled with international students, poor and working-class residents, immigrants and people of color, and members with languages, religions, genders, and ethnicities too many to enumerate. That diversity evaporated once you looked higher up the ladders of representation. When I was hired in 2003, there was only one person of color on NASCO's board of directors. I was gobsmacked. So were the members. But this was a cooperative, and, therefore, democratic, participatory change was baked into the governance structure. We could do something about it.

In 2003, a discontented coalition made up of NASCO's queer caucus and its people of color caucus drafted a Plan for Inclusion. This was a set of thirteen proposals, great and small, that would shift power and representation for racial justice inside our association. The proposals ranged from small things like including presenters of color in NASCO's conference programming on racial equity to structural changes in governance like appointing a representative from the people of color caucus to the board and ensuring a minimum of three folks of color on the board. Members at that year's annual general meeting approved small changes, such as ensuring there were more Black and Brown keynote speakers, but rejected every structural measure. Resistance was strongest among whiter co-ops in Ontario and in the Midwest. A multiracial subset of our members was enraged at the obstruction of the handful of co-ops with white leadership and disproportionate voting power that thwarted progress. As director of education and the only Black staffer, I was disheartened and angry. Nevertheless, I had perspective on the story behind these votes.

My job involved year-round relationship building. I would crisscross the US and southern Ontario delivering trainings on cooperative skills like facilitation and decision-making to help hired and elected leaders better steward their co-ops. This experience meant that even though I felt betrayed, I had insight into the trepidation with which those delegates cast their votes. My colleagues in the caucuses were ready to fight. Our shared goal was the implementation of this Plan for Inclusion, but we disagreed on how to make that happen. They said that if we tried to force this change and failed, they would rather go down fighting, having changed nothing, and secede from the association with righteous dignity. I appealed to them to play the long game and see if I could get through to the dissenters.

That spring, I convinced a slightly more diverse but still overwhelmingly white board to approve an organizing project. The pitch was to fund me to drive around Ohio, Michigan, Ontario, and Wisconsin to do racial equity education. This was the beginning of our win. It enabled me to spend that summer sitting down in smaller, more relaxed settings to help leadership within the powerful dissenting co-ops understand the principles behind sharing power.

I dispelled racist rhetoric about quotas, and we talked about the solidarity of the white delegates entrusting their voting power to endorse what the coalition was proposing, even if the white delegates didn't fully understand the broader analysis of the problem—let alone the proposed structural solutions. I struggled to find a delicate way to illustrate that it was arrogant and narcissistic for their bloc to insist that change had to wait until they felt fully caught up in understanding systems of oppression. Even if they couldn't grasp the motivations of their fellow members, surely it was clear that marginalized co-op members felt hurt and angry, that this didn't feel cooperative to them or to me.

I connected this disenfranchisement to the reality that these dissenting co-ops actually had the power to leverage their votes and change conditions. That latter point really stuck with them. In a world with so much injustice—recall that the backdrop was the Blair and Bush administrations' invasion of Iraq in spite of millions mobilizing worldwide against that war—it's absolutely critical that we use whatever power we have to do what is right and help a righteous cause.

Something finally clicked. These leaders didn't want to be the Bush administration of our progressive cooperative association. Proposals in the Plan for Inclusion were ardently adopted at that fall's annual meeting, four months after my visits to a handful of student co-ops with disproportionate power.

Lacking a sober assessment of our options, my resistance-oriented friends from the member caucuses had been prepared to fight, lose, and withdraw their membership from the association rather than consider effective ways to win in the long run. In fact, one allied co-op did leave, which made it more difficult to get the votes necessary to adopt the Plan for Inclusion.

My experience both talking and fighting as a campus organizer at University of California, Berkeley, gave me the perspective necessary to realize that this was a battle we could win through patience and dialogue. When I left NASCO after three years on staff and seven years on the board, there wasn't a single straight cis white man on the board of directors. We had long since elected the first cohort of trans and nonbinary board members, supported by queer women of color, single moms, and Muslim students, who all brought a new leadership culture to that network.

I understand how the stark injustice of our society compels us to insist on fighting. Movement culture is so entrenched in opposition that it is usually pretty hard to let go of our adversarial stance to explore negotiation. That is just as true in the work of transformative justice when the time comes to interact with our comrades in changemaking as it is when we're in the ring with our opponents.[2] The world being unjust, activists understandably identify as rebels, outcasts, and revolutionaries. When our primary recourse is to "resist," we find ourselves in situations where the choice to obstruct usually seems strategic. In that context, we may misidentify a potential ally as an opponent, or we may default to fighting even when we win a seat at the very table where our voice is needed to seize power or redirect it.

Most of that opposition and advocacy is good. Our world needs more fighters and a stronger resistance, but fighting is really only a means. Only when we take a moment to reflect does it become clear that justice is only our motivation; our liberation is the goal. We can't confuse the fight itself for the goal. Deep, transformative change requires good strategy, and it turns out our movements are a little short on practices for developing it.

Rebecca and I have had a chance to advise fights and to work on negotiations together. In these pages you will find the language that I've started to learn as she introduces it to clients who are organizers and activists. You'll see how the wisest groups don't jump into their strategy with a foregone conclusion about their approach. They ask, "What is the strategic and principled path through talking and fighting that will build our power and bring us wins along the way?"

I agree with Rebecca that strategy decisions tend to be based on four factors: power dynamics, structural barriers that limit your choice of action, principles, and biases that groups have about whether to appease or to antagonize. These factors complement what I believe are guiding inputs for effective strategy: vision, historical and material analysis, future orientation, and emergence. Put them together and you have a particularly juicy set of ideas for organizers to play with.

Communities organizing for transformation need first-rate strategy tools. We need more love, wit, and smarts in our movements for change. Love and logic are each other's mistress. They are the two handrails that can guide us to justice. You'll read Rebecca's story illustrating some of the ways that love, logic, justice, and facilitation are part of the labor of changemaking. These shaped her design of the dozen tools woven into this book—which I hope you will employ in our struggles for freedom.

Philadelphia, PA
February 2020

Foreword

Douglas Stone

For the past thirty years, I've written about and taught conflict resolution and have been a practitioner in the field. I see the work I do as a kind of corrective to the narrative that in order to survive human beings have evolved to fight. Sure, we evolved to fight, I point out, but we also evolved to cooperate; when disputes arise, we have the capacity to handle them without violence or aggression and sometimes even with compassion and altruism.

Now comes Rebecca's book, which, even with my biases toward talk, I see as a groundbreaking corrective to the corrective.

Let's take a few steps back. I came to this work as a student and then colleague of Roger Fisher, one of the grandfathers of the field of conflict resolution, and a coauthor of *Getting to Yes*, the seminal book about "interest-based negotiation," which first appeared in 1981. Roger was an evangelist; he asserted that while conflict was inevitable, managing it well could not only prevent wasteful and destructive lawsuits but could sometimes prevent war. As a pilot in World War II, he had seen war's ravages up close and, upon returning home, dedicated his life to finding better ways to manage differences—whether between countries, organizations, significant others, or community members.

Roger taught that the best way for a person to manage conflict was by listening to others with an open heart and genuine curiosity and working creatively (and collaboratively, when possible) to develop solutions that might satisfy the interests of all parties. Before *Getting to Yes*, the dominant model of dealing with conflict was "win-lose." The game went like this: if you are loud, you win, and if you are soft, you lose. If you are strong, you win, and if you are weak, you lose. If you like conflict, you win, and if you don't, you lose. Under these rules, a lot of us had lost before the game even started.

Fisher's method offered the possibility of "win-win" outcomes and gave hope to those of us who avoided conflict or lacked resources.[1] In my own work in conflict and change, I was astounded by how helpful good conflict management skills could be. Time and again, people would engage us, claiming they'd reached the end of the line; they had tried everything, but the situation was beyond repair. What else could be done? Plenty, usually. Like Roger, I'm an evangelist for the benefits of talking and understanding. I believe passionately that although talking may not always resolve a conflict or bring about needed social change, it almost always helps.

This can be a tough sell. In the United States, we are increasingly polarized, with more of us planting ourselves at the extremes on key issues and fewer of us making our way to the middle. How can we collaborate if we can't even agree on what the challenges are, what is or is not real, and what did or did not happen? Angry and fearful—and burning for change *now*—we wonder if the time for talk has passed.

There's an upside to polarization, anger, and fear; they mobilize us toward action. When we are angry or afraid, and when we have moral clarity about who the enemy is, we are more likely to organize, vote, donate, march, or disrupt. We are more likely to *fight*, to use Rebecca's encompassing word, for what matters most to us. In *Rules for Radicals*, Saul Alinsky observed of the rhetoric around the American Revolution: "Our cause had to be all shining justice, allied with the angels; theirs had to be all evil, tied to the Devil; in no war has the enemy or the cause ever been gray."[2] As we become angrier or more fearful, gray washes away, and our resolve for action strengthens.

But there are downsides to anger and fear. Politicians, media personalities, and corporate and religious leaders on all sides can manipulate our anger and fear to motivate us to fight for what matters most to *them*. Meanwhile, anger and fear can diminish our interest in understanding others and dampen our thirst for reconciliation. Another downside, I would argue, is that if we are not careful, these emotions can put us on the pernicious path toward dehumanization. I do not need to work to understand those on the other side, because I *already* understand them; they are wrong, and they are evil—in short, they are a cartoon, which is to say, not human.

In my work, I've observed that it is harder to hate or fear people you've had a meaningful conversation with, people whose hopes and dreams you have come to know, people whose life victories and childhood wounds you have taken the time to learn about. In the absence of meaningful and direct conversations, a downward spiral can form; less communication leads to more anger and fear, which leads to greater polarization, which leads to even less communication, which leads to even more anger and fear, more polarization, and so on. The failure to communicate is both cause and effect of greater polarization. (None of this is to say, by the way, that anger, fear, and polarization are *only* caused by poor communication. Far from it. The claim here is that poor communication makes already deep and challenging divides deeper and more challenging.)

Nonetheless, it is reasonable to ask: If you seek a fundamental shift in policy—on climate change, for example—is talking really going to get the job done? How about when your unarmed neighbor is shot by the cops, or the school you send your child to is underfunded? Or maybe you consider abortion murder or believe everyone should have access to health care or want something done about the chaos on the US-Mexico border or find the prospect of continued mass incarceration horrifying or have a friend who died of opioid addiction, because there was no money to fund treatment. Maybe you fear that more social programs will bankrupt the country or are sick of listening to billionaires whine about tax increases while so many people are living on the streets. Should we have more chitchat, or should we *do* something?

Sometimes talking resolves or manages conflict in good ways. My tendency, all things being equal, is to urge more talking. But I have come to believe that the analysis is more complicated—that for all the benefits of talking and all the drawbacks of fighting, more talk isn't *always* the better course. Sometimes meaningful change—whatever the change you seek—*requires* organized resistance, disruption, and maybe—*maybe*—even violence. If we can do damage by failing to talk, we can also do damage by failing to fight.

When should we do which?

This is exactly the question this book so brilliantly answers. If the book does its job, we will step back from our comfortable default assumptions about how to engage and, instead, consider our purposes, context, and history, the relationship between ends and means, power dynamics and power asymmetries, and the benefits and drawbacks of a range of ways to engage. I am hopeful that fewer of us will choose to fight only because that's all we know or choose talking because we fear confrontation. Instead, with Rebecca's guidance, we will make thoughtful choices based on clearheaded analyses of possible outcomes and short- and longer-term consequences. We will resort to disruption only when we have exhausted all other viable choices, but we will not avoid disruption just for the sake of quiet. Maybe we will no longer see talking and fighting as opposites or exclusive of each other. Perhaps those who are talking can be making plans for what a fight would look like, and those who are fighting can coordinate with the other side to be talking simultaneously (or eventually).

Before my conversations with Rebecca, I didn't spend much time thinking about how to help people make smart choices between talking and fighting, but Rebecca has taught me that helping people think clearly about these choices is part of my role. Her book gives me and all of us the framework we need to make wise choices.

In this way, Rebecca's analysis of when to fight makes a crucial contribution to the cause of peace.

Cambridge, MA
February 2020

Preface

I submitted the manuscript of this book in March 2020, just as the COVID-19 pandemic began to cross the United States. The new uprising for Black lives started in May, and Donald Trump lost the election in November. Now it is March 2021, and *When to Talk and When to Fight* is going to press. Yet the forces of 2020 still have mighty sway. This is a terrible time to be a person. Black people are in pain, immigrants are in pain, workers, children, and parents are in pain. White nationalists are retrenching. No one is immune to the spreading bleakness of hurricanes, fires, unprecedented winter storms, and despair. Now, in the US and worldwide, we face strategic choices exactly like the ones described in the pages that follow.

In this context, activists and changemakers need a language to strategize with one another. I hope the model introduced in this book is useful in creating plans of action when the stakes are as high as they are today.

> Can't you see it
> I know you can feel it
> It's all in the air
> I can't stand the pressure much longer
> Somebody say a prayer.
> —Nina Simone, 1964

Philadelphia, PA
February 2021

Author's Notes

A few names have been changed to keep my testimony as unlikely as feasible to provoke disconcert among my community and family members: Cody the organizer, Dana who taught me to smoke a cigarette, my first lover Linda, her soldier Taubman, and my colleague Malek.

I use the pronoun "they" to refer to people unless I know they use the pronouns "he" or "she" or something else.

I minimize the use of words describing what healthy eyes do, e.g., "seeing" and "looking," to increase the accessibility of my metaphors to people with impaired vision.

Black and Brown are capitalized when I refer to people's racial identities. There are many views on this topic, but I want to show respect for the self-definition by Black and Brown people as Black and Brown and acknowledge the history of the racialization by white people of Black and Brown people. I would be inclined to capitalize White too, because "white" as a racial identity ought to be distinguished from "white" as a hue. It's as impressionist a description of Americans of Irish, Ashkenazi Jewish, Italian, and Greek heritage as Black is of African Americans. But "White" is an uncommon usage, and I don't want to distract readers by suggesting I have something special to say by using it.

You will run into a few words in the book containing "ch" or "kh" in Arabic, Hebrew, or Yiddish transliterations. Each of these spellings represents a version of the hard "h" of a fish bone caught in your throat.

I created a bibliography and removed it after I counted the number of Black, Indigenous, people of color, women, and transgender authors whose books I had listed. There are over one hundred endnotes to the book, and I noticed how much more racial and gender diversity they contained than the bibliography of published books. Removing the bibliography was a way to raise up the primacy of music, poetry, film, news media, journals, and other sources where the barriers to publication may be less exclusive than the barriers to publishing a book.

Nevertheless, you will note that most of the experts and academics cited in this book are white men, while the anecdotes are about people of all racial and gender identities. I don't know more white men than anyone else, but I, like you perhaps, have studied the writing of more white men. That is a reality of our culture, with rank and power playing the roles that they do in raising the profile of work and thinking. I ask you to keep that in mind as you read, since I have done nothing to correct it except write this book.

A NEW ABC FOR UNDERSTANDING CONFLICT

■ CHAPTER 1

Lovers and Fighters: A Personal Story

Imagine there's no countries
It isn't hard to do
Nothing to kill or die for
And no religion, too
Imagine all the people
Living life in peace
—John Lennon[1]

We Have All Experienced Conflict

Every one of us has experienced conflict. If you haven't had fights with your siblings, you've struggled with your parents or broken up a fight among someone's kids. If you haven't gone head-to-head with a landlord, you've probably haggled with a real estate agent. You may have mobilized coworkers against your boss, fought in a war or marched against one, negotiated a business deal, or made up with your spouse.

You may have grown up around constant arguing. You may be the survivor of childhood battles with abusive adults. Maybe you have come up against the criminal justice system or maybe you are part of it. Every day may be a fight for you, facing a world built to suit some people but not most people.

Experiences like these, along with your own personal inclinations and beliefs, inform your response to conflict. You may be drawn to overthrow our socioeconomic system with its steady production of inequality, injustice, and destruction. You may be drawn to the strategic, tactical, and mentally challenging aspects of conflict or to the balance of analytic and emotional challenges that negotiation and deal-making require.

You might identify with others aligned in social struggle or change, whether as an organizer, campaigner, movement builder, or revolutionary. You may be a union member who's been on strike or a labor negotiator or a manager. You might be a lawyer or a professional mediator.

Besides that, you may even take a public stand for your favored approach to conflict. Your email signature might read, "Those who profess to favor freedom, and yet depreciate agitation, are men who want crops without plowing up the ground," courtesy of abolitionist Frederick Douglass.[2] Your bike may have a bumper sticker with this quote from the Dalai Lama: "Be kind whenever possible. It is always possible."[3]

To some readers, all of these approaches to conflict and social change may be appealing, but most of you probably have favorites. Whether we are mediators, managers, politicians, academics, students, or social change activists, some of us prefer to build power, while others would rather solve problems directly with our would-be opponents. When it comes to making change in society, in our communities, or in the organizations in which we make our individual contributions, some changemakers spend most of their time in dialogue; others mobilize for protest.

When to Talk and When to Fight is a conversation among these groups and their approaches to conflict. It is about the different preferences, values, and analyses that lead them to different choices at critical moments on the path to change.

Conflict is when your people want something, and the other side isn't giving it up. Conflict emerges at the moment your side needs to decide whether to struggle to build power or sit down to negotiate with the other side: whether to talk or to fight. This book is for people who are drawn to moments of conflict—to struggles, campaigns, and fights at work and in our communities. It is about these moments of choice, whether your inclination is to fight and win or to find resolution without destroying relationships or ruining lives.

A New Language for Conflict Strategy

When it comes to handling conflict, sometimes talking makes more strategic sense than fighting, and sometimes fighting is a more promising strategy. In some settings, one might perceive fighting as morally wrong and, in others, as the only principled course. In addition to questions of strategy and principle, most of us have preferences, comfort zones, and even biases toward either dialogue or resistance. Some people are natural provocateurs. To others, peacemaking is a more natural choice.

In 2016, as public attention to the killings of Black people by police rose, San Francisco 49ers quarterback Colin Kaepernick was moved to act. He decided to "take a knee" during the playing of the national anthem before the team's games. Kaepernick says he had gotten "to the point where I knew it was the right thing to do. I knew I had to stand up for people who aren't being treated fairly, and I felt strongly enough about that to be willing to take that risk." Sportswriter Howard Bryant further explained Kaepernick's strategy:

> It was the gesture that directed the country's attention toward the police and a justice system completely unwilling to convict officers whose use of deadly force seemed to be the first and only option in confrontations with African American citizens. "I am not going to stand up to show pride in a flag for a country that oppresses black people and people of color," Kaepernick said. . . . "There are bodies in the street and people getting paid leave and getting away with murder."[4]

Black athletes, wrote Bryant, are usually expected to be peacemakers, urging calm in the face of blatant racism and engaging white owners and fans in dialogue. But Kaepernick, he argued, "is not a peacemaker. He did not seek the approval of the white public for his beliefs. He did not try to make them comfortable. There were no ride-alongs with cops or PR experts massaging the words until they found *just the right tone* that didn't offend the mainstream or the cops."[5] Witnessing Kaepernick's action, the National Football League, President Trump, and half the public were indeed offended.

Taking a knee was only one of several responses by NFL players to the newly elevated profile of anti-Black police violence. The Philadelphia Eagles' Malcolm Jenkins and others raised a fist during the national anthem. Then Jenkins and a group of fellow athletes decided to form the Players Coalition, whose goal was "to secure resources from billionaire owners to create change."[6] Jenkins and other members of the Players Coalition had already shown they were willing, even eager, to fight, but in forming the Coalition, they becoming peacemakers and dialogue leaders. Their new strategy was to encourage the NFL to save face by funding equality-oriented causes rather than anger league management with displays of disobedience in the name of equality and justice. Through negotiation with the NFL, the

Players Coalition helped create an $89 million fund to address criminal justice reform. They also stayed in the good graces of league management.[7]

Meanwhile, over on the soccer field, white superstar Megan Rapinoe explained why she had copied Kaepernick's kneeling protest:

> I haven't experienced over-policing, racial profiling, police brutality or the sight of a family member's body lying dead in the street. But I cannot stand idly by while there are people in this country who have had to deal with that kind of heartache. . . . I have chosen to kneel because not two miles from my hotel in Columbus, Ohio, on the night before our match against Thailand, a 13-year-old boy named Tyre King was fatally shot by a police officer. . . . I know that actions must be taken to help bring about real change. Right now, I am reaching out to community leaders, corporate partners and leaders within the Black Lives Matter movement to figure out all the ways I can best support the efforts already in motion. . . . If you are in a position of influence like I am, you can use your platform to elevate the millions of voices being silenced, and support them in the tremendous work already being done.

Rapinoe chose both approaches to conflict—talking as well as fighting. In taking a knee, Rapinoe chose an in-your-face approach, violating the norms of professional sports. She then went on to advocate dialogue between privileged white people like herself and Black and Brown people facing police brutality: "Having these kinds of conversations can be difficult and complex, but so what? We should talk to our family members and challenge them, bringing these hard problems to the dinner table and persevering through uncomfortable conversations."[8]

Kaepernick and other players fought while the Players Coalition negotiated. Rapinoe herself both fought and encouraged dialogue. Sometimes parallel tracks for dialogue and protest can strengthen a group's position, but not all groups are open to both approaches. Similarly, it can make good sense for a group to fight a more powerful opponent for a place at the table, and then jointly negotiate a resolution. But not all groups move strategically between talking and fighting as the balance of power shifts.

To everything there is a season—a time for talking with our opponents and a time for fighting to win. This book is about the ways communities, movements, and organizations face change, deal with division, make deals, and change systems. You will be introduced to an easy-to-learn model for talking across the modalities of negotiation and resistance. The model will help groups that prefer one or the other approach and communities that study and teach one or the other approach to have useful and coherent conversations with each other.

This model is as simple as A, B, C, with all conflict activity divided into three buckets: talking, fighting for power, and fighting to vanquish an opponent.

Over the course of my seven years teaching an undergraduate philosophy course called "The Problem of War" and twice as many years teaching "Introduction to Peace and Conflict Studies," the ABC model practically created itself. With my colleagues at Dragonfly Partners, I have used the model for many years to better understand the decisions facing the advocacy groups we advise and support. I believe it is useful for many people—expert negotiators and superstar organizers, candidates for office and revolutionaries, new students and old teachers—in decoding historical conflict and analyzing the dilemmas we face today.

The book isn't here to moralize or change behavior; it's here to offer new language for what we already do. It answers questions, including: How can we talk about peace and justice coherently in a single conversation? What can an analysis of purpose, power, and principle tell us about why a group has chosen either to talk or to fight in a given situation? How can we cross-pollinate the wisdom of negotiators and social changemakers—and, in so doing, expand our strategic repertoires?

When to Talk and When to Fight contains a new way of understanding and discussing the limits and possibilities of each approach to conflict. We'll deep-dive into the dynamics of power among groups in conflict, as well as the strategic implications for choosing talking or fighting. We'll examine the values and principles that guide a group toward either talking or fighting and provide examples of the habits, biases, and structural barriers that may limit or determine the choices a group makes when facing an apparently formidable opponent.

My own habits of conflict emerged from the host of experiences that I have faced across six decades of life and work. In the end, and since the beginning, I claim dual loyalty to talking and fighting.

Traditions

My family's particular blend of tradition and morality was a version of Orthodox Judaism with its own stubborn character. One tradition I grew up with was that my family disapproved of fighting. We were as polite as Presbyterians and compliant, but we were also nonconformist, even peculiar. Our way may not have been the way of everyone else, or, for that matter, *anyone* else, but my siblings and I were taught that it was the only right way. There were rules for every facet of childhood existence. To inhabit this world safely, most people followed the rules. But as the youngest of four, I had a little extra legroom.

If memories are replays, I have watched this one the most: I recall myself at age three, riding my beloved rocking horse on the Sabbath, known to us as *shabbes*. Writing of any kind was forbidden on this holy day, and I knew better than to scribble on my toys. But I remember taking a crayon to the saddle of my horse and being rewarded with divine impunity. I had never seen a member of my family knowingly disobey Jewish law; we were the obedient grandchildren of immigrants, guided by order within unambiguous boundaries. Yet those boundaries had captured my attention; I had violated the "no writing on shabbes" rule, and nothing had happened—no lightning bolts, no yelling from God, no consequences. It was the first of many times in my life that I made a run for the boundaries.

The lives of the people around us did not seem as prescribed as ours were. Yes, like me, my friends were all youngest in their families. Like mine, their parents were born before World War II to Eastern European Jewish families that had settled in the Great Lakes manufacturing city of Rochester, New York. Like my family, theirs had some version of synagogue, kosher food, and shabbes observance. As we grew to be preteens, my friends, like me, kissed boys and then each other, as we copied their hippie siblings and lived into the spirit of liberated 1970s white America.

On our seventh-grade class trip to Niagara Falls in 1972, we asked the fortune-telling machine at the Ripley's Believe It or Not Museum which of us would be married first, and then we all swore we'd never marry. We were only thirteen years old at the time, but, unlike my friends, I thought we meant it, and, through bends in the road and back again, wound up a bona fide devotee to free love.

Freedom was not as serious and urgent a political pursuit for them as it was for me. If my own older siblings did any rebelling, it was too subtle for me to perceive. There just wasn't space in the family to do it. I had more cover as the youngest, but I also had more need for cover. As a tomboy, I cringed inside the constraints of gender convention. By the time my siblings abandoned me for college, my parents were relaxed enough about child-rearing that I could easily perceive the contradictions between their old-school rules and the urgency of liberation that was our legacy from the sixties.

Don't get me wrong: my family was full of implied love and intellectual delight, camping trips and Scrabble games, and, most importantly, unconditional endorsement of us kids as people. There was always singing, whether Hebrew prayers or Yiddish, Zionist, and American folk songs. But when strict parents, however nonconformist, produce a nonconforming child, there's trouble.

Learning to Talk

I am a transmasculine anti-Zionist able-bodied white American Ashkenazi secular Jewish mom, or that is how I would identify myself if I were thirty. I am twice that, so it takes more words to explain my passage from a religious Zionist world to this one.

As fourth child of four, it was no surprise that I became an extrovert. I was the fourth child to be one of the smartest in their class, fourth elected to office in the National Conference of Synagogue Youth (or NCSY), fourth to be a national merit finalist, fourth to be inducted into NCSY's Ben Zakkai Honor Society. But I was first to do it all with a focus on political advocacy.

I had inherited a mishmash of traditional and liberal political views. My parents voted for civil rights and against the Vietnam War, but they opposed socialism and, very naturally, supported Israel. My mother was unemployed during the Nixon administration's Watergate hearings and watched every hour of them, reporting over 6:00 p.m. supper on the soliloquies of her favorite senators.

Such was the blend of conservative and contemporary inside our house at 11 Tarrytown Road. Beyond the moral boundary lay the improper and the unacceptable—no eating without a blessing, no talking with food in your mouth, no interrupting. No mercy for Neville Chamberlain, the UK's famous appeaser of Adolf Hitler. Chamberlain had made concessions to Hitler in the 1938 Munich Accord to avoid bringing the UK into the war unprepared. It was the same strategy the biblical Jacob had used to placate his brother Esau. Evidently, sometimes fighting was called for.

The Soviet Union was inscribed twice on the 11 Tarrytown bad list, once for being communist and again for its mistreatment of Jews. In the case of the Jews for Jesus, I saw my father's intermittent intolerance head-on. Some of my NCSY friends had hatched a plan to infiltrate the Jews for

Jesus. I sent away for an LP of Jews for Jesus tunes to use in our opposition research. To me this was holy work, but when my dad found out, he made me break the record in two. I had brought controversy inside the house. As it says in Ecclesiastes, there is a time to keep and a time to cast away.

Julius and Ethel Rosenberg, put to death by the US Congress in 1953 for passing state secrets to the Soviet Union, were on the bad list. The civil rights leader Andrew Young was good; my mother loved an eloquent public speaker. Politician Barbara Jordan was good too. Monthly issues of the *Saturday Review* were piled up tidily on an end table, and its editor, the nuclear weapons opponent Norman Cousins, could do no wrong. On the other end table was a book called *Lightning Out of Israel* about the 1967 Israeli-Arab war, a baby-faced soldier on the cover gazing dreamily at Jerusalem's Western Wall. Generally, if someone was on the bad list, it was better not to discuss it. I am quite sure Abbie Hoffman was suspect, but the Black Panthers were terribly wrong. We did not discuss them.

As I grew into early adulthood, I would take both the pro-justice and pro-Israel fierceness from my family, drop the moderation, and turn up the heat.

Starting to Fight

In ninth grade, Mr. Lutterbein, who taught our Criminal and Civil Law elective, took us on a field trip to watch the US Federal Court in session. We rode a chartered bus west from Rochester to Buffalo, bypassing the little village of Attica, New York.

Three years earlier, Governor Nelson Rockefeller had called out state troopers to put down a prison rebellion at the Attica Correctional Facility; in the process troops killed twenty-nine prisoners and ten guards. Inmates had taken hostages, demanding better prison conditions as part of a national movement against deadly racist prison policies. Once the air cleared, more than sixty surviving prisoners were prosecuted in connection with the rebellion. It was one of these trials that we attended in Buffalo.

After watching the court proceedings, we walked through the snow from the federal building to a storefront where the Attica Brothers Legal Defense Fund did its support work. Some of the volunteers for the Attica Brothers had been at court that day, along with their famous lawyer William Kunstler, and we all walked back to the storefront office together. We learned quickly that the thirty- and forty-year-old men helping us fourteen-year-olds climb over the Buffalo snowbanks were former Attica inmates. The man who took my arm to keep us both from slipping told me that he had done time for murder. Now they were all raising money to defend their prison brothers for standing up to the system.

When it was time to get on the bus, we said goodbye and walked to the door, passing a table piled with political literature. I saw a stack of pamphlets titled *Palestinian National Covenant*. I picked one up. On the back it said, "published by the Weather Underground." I knew this was anti-Israel material and—as we saw it at the time—deeply antisemitic propaganda, and I didn't want anyone else to see it! So I took as many copies as I thought I could get away with and stashed them in my book bag. To me, every copy I grabbed represented one potential recruit to antisemitism sabotaged.

Walking arm in arm with a murderer had made me feel warm and brave. Stealing the pile of propaganda made me feel proud and scared. I was a bit naughty, but, in my heart, my choices of action were in the service of loving all the people—ex-prisoners, criminal defendants, and anti-racist rabble-rousers, even if they were antisemites—every bit as much as my community of Jewish supporters of Israel, and every bit as much as I loved my God.

In tenth grade, I set up a formal debate on Israel for the grown-ups in our synagogue. We invited Mayor Stephen May to moderate a debate between Merwin Kroll, a leader at the Jewish Community Federation of Rochester, and Dr. Aly Nahas, who was president of the Arab American Society of Rochester and father of two kids at my school. A Muslim Arab and a non-observant Jew, with the Christian mayor as moderator—I was both a natural provocateur and an eager peacemaker.

When I was in eleventh grade, the movement in solidarity with Jews in the Soviet Union was in high gear. I flew to Brussels to represent NCSY at a conference organized to raise the profile of the struggle for religious freedom and for the rights of Jews to leave the USSR. It was a meeting of adults, and I was the youngest delegate, so I stayed close to the twenty-somethings from the Student Struggle for Soviet Jewry. One of their leaders, Rabbi Avi Weiss, was a rising star in the world of Orthodox Jewish social activism.

The conference ended on a Friday, and many of the attendees went to Amsterdam for shabbes. The religious adults who let me tag along with them paid in advance for our Saturday lunch at Mouwes Kosher Restaurant, since we were prohibited from exchanging money on shabbes. As our little group rehashed the conference over our meal, talking about our canal ride the day before and singing our shabbes songs, Rabbi Avi Weiss recognized us from his table. Looking like any man in my family with a dress shirt for shabbes and a crocheted yarmulke bobby-pinned to the top of his head, he walked over, accompanied by a woman dressed in layers of colorful patchwork. The buttons on her sweater were misaligned, each fastened to the wrong partner. She was so familiar! A messy oddball Jewish American hippie freak in a skirt, smiling warmly at me. Rabbi Avi Weiss introduced us to his sister. I thought, "He and she are both me! Which is me? Which am I? Who am I??"

Back and forth, back and forth I went, bridging worlds and studying them. When I was a kid, the women of our household started off to synagogue at 9:30 on Saturday mornings. My job was to holler up the stairs to my grandmother's kitchen: "Bubbie, we're ready to go to shul." "Your mother is ready?" "Yeah." "Rebecca, the word is not *yeah*. It's *yes*." Sit like a lady, legs together, shoulders back, don't hunch. This was the work of a grandchild of working-class immigrants, even a tomboy grandchild.

If I was fourth of four for the good stuff, I was first for the signposts of disobedience: first to play spin the bottle in eighth grade, first to steal the keys to the shul youth lounge, first to get an F in high school Shakespeare. Lots of my transgressions happened with or because of my friend Dana. She kissed boys and smoked pot, maybe because her older sister was the most rebellious of all our siblings. One day at Dana's house, she closed the bedroom door and taught me how to smoke a cigarette. A couple years later, I smoked my second cigarette with a man guarding the welcome booth of a kibbutz in the Galilee; I was eighteen, in Israel to study the Jewish texts, and I had walked into this kibbutz on a solo hitchhiking trip.

My third cigarette came later the same year when my roommate Linda doubted the kibbutz cigarette story and dared me to show her how I held one. She was experienced in sex and drugs, and her Crosby, Stills and Nash and Rod Stewart tapes were the soundtrack for our gap year.

Linda had had sex with a boy called Taubman who came to visit us in Jerusalem. Taubman looked sharp in his Israel Defense Forces uniform, and later Linda teased me about me wanting sex with Taubman, because she knew I wanted to learn sex. It wasn't long before Linda and I started frolicking in the sleeping bag ourselves.

My accumulating transgressions weighed heavily on my mind, and I badly needed a course correction to keep from losing track of myself. The course correction came at twenty-one, but I lost track of myself regardless.

I was in my last year at Barnard College in New York, finishing my degree in politics and writing. My crowd was religious Jews, and it was easy to date boys, but it was really hard to make sense of all the strands of me.

Before marrying the rabbi who would father my two children, I was obliged to attend *kallah* class. This is where brides learn about sex and the ritual laws. The teacher gave me a pamphlet with a mustard yellow cover and all the important details inside. The traditional rituals obligate a wife to predict the onset of menstruation to prevent accidental contact between a person with their period and a Jewish husband. There were no online spreadsheets or apps, but that would have helped; you had to use a complex period prediction system to avoid a spiritually costly error like sleeping in the same bed, or touching at all—even handing the baby back and forth was against the rules—while you were bleeding. If you hadn't had the same span of days between periods for at least three months running, you had to take precautionary space from your mate on three dates: twenty-eight days since you last bled, a lunar month, and the last month's interval, just in case.

There was more to kallah class than that. To determine when your period is officially over, you have to pay attention to the color of your vaginal discharge. If it's lighter than the mustard color of the kallah class pamphlet, you can start counting seven days, pay a visit to the ritual bath, the *mikva*, and go home, with any luck, to a vase of flowers and the kids tucked in for the night. If you do the math, you'll notice that mikva night has a good chance of coinciding with ovulation—which is why, as I said, we wound up with two kids.

If it comes to pass that you issue a discharge of an iffy color, you may need to consult an expert. I only had to do this once: I put a pair of underpants in an interoffice envelope and sent it via intersettlement delivery to the head rabbi of our community. I can't remember how he got the verdict back to me or what it was, but I do remember that there was some leeway in the system for the owner of the underpants to make their own determination. If, like me, you were not looking forward to going home on mikva night, you might have your own very special interpretation of what color was on that bit of white cotton.

The settlement community I'm referring to was Katif, in the Gaza Strip. When we fulfilled our religious commitment of moving to our people's homeland, Gaza was a natural place to land. Israel and Egypt had signed a peace treaty in 1979, and many of the Jews from settlements in the northern Sinai Peninsula, now Egyptian territory, had found new homes just inside Israeli-controlled Gaza.

Life in the all-Jewish village of Katif was idyllic for a couple of religious hippies. Our little plaster house sat in the sand dunes, and, as new immigrants, the government of Israel paid most of our rent. The settlers had built a beautiful palm-leaf partition, a *mechitzah*, from the shore down into the Mediterranean to separate the Jewish men's and women's beaches. The men took turns guarding the barbed-wire fence that surrounded Katif, but I don't remember worrying too much about safety. We ordered produce from the neighboring Palestinian village of Khan Yunis, and, one time, in the quantity column, I indicated that I wanted one head of garlic—or so I thought. I got one, alright—one kilo, a long beautiful braid of garlic heads, which decorated my Katif kitchen and our next kitchen in Jerusalem until we flew back to the United States for good.

The stress of accumulated contradictions crossed the ocean with me—contradictions between liberal American values and direct experience of the Israeli-Palestinian reality, between 1970s cultural messages of freedom and universalism and the constrictions of religious orthodoxy, and between my experiences of gender and sexuality and the expectations of my socially conservative family and community. Multiplying the stress was my deeply troubled marriage.

From Jerusalem, my family moved to Los Angeles, where I left my husband. The lesbian problem didn't consciously factor into my decision, and the religion problem got a free ride out too. I left because my husband didn't treat me right. He hurt my body and my psyche. Four years and two children into our marriage, I drove away on a Saturday morning, the first time in my life that I had been in a car before sundown on shabbes.

This was a very long ride across the San Fernando Valley. In the car, I wasn't brave enough to remove the headscarf that signified my married status, but I was ready to make two other declarations to myself: I was now an atheist, and I could shed the pretense of accepting the validity of Israel as an ethnically defined state. The rest of the changes came in waves.

The effects of trauma on a life are great. Old wounds make it easy for a person to feel, to think, and, sometimes, to act in solidarity with others who have suffered the trauma of being hit, raped, pushed aside, unseen. They increase our sensitivity to tension and the need to choose how we will interact with the sources of that tension. For many, trauma is a powerful motivator, feeding the urge to change the world around us.

All Out for the Cause

I came out in layers. I was twenty-five when I landed in New York City with my babies and took a computer job at Citibank. I learned to be a nonreligious person in New York City, which is to say, not really a Jew at all, as far as I was concerned. Adam was my boss and had the same SAT scores as me. Troy was handsome and talked about driving to California to plant a vineyard. Adam and Troy got high every day after work. They invited me to join in; I only did it once or twice, and I hardly inhaled. I was new at everything!

Here was another new thing: in the cubicle next to mine sat a consultant named David. He'd been a magazine model before he learned programming, and he was older than the rest of us. David showed us centerfold pictures of himself. I didn't fully understand that. Was he actually gay? This seemed to me on the edge of unreal.

From lower Manhattan, I would take the D train to Brooklyn, do a grocery shop and pick up laundry, then head to East 21st Street, where the teenager Debbie Cohen was in our apartment watching the kids. I had met Debbie's mother at a Parents Without Partners meeting. Getting off the subway at Kings Highway on Fridays, I remember being afraid that the Metropolitan Transit Authority cops would arrest me for riding the train on shabbes. There was a Wendy's under the Kings Highway train trestle, and I took that Wendy's in stages. First I ate a hamburger, featuring nonkosher meat. Then I had a cheeseburger, featuring the prohibited meat in prohibited combination with a dairy product. Finally, I ate a bacon cheeseburger.

I learned one new thing after another. Troy invited me to his New Year's party in Manhattan, and I got drunk and high, and someone showed me how to snort cocaine. To seem like I had friends, I had told Troy that I was going to another party first. Where I actually went was to the Gay and Lesbian Community Services Center on West 13th Street, where I peeked into a big room with a band playing and booze and hundreds of strangers flirting and dancing. I stayed in the hallway and read the flyers on the bulletin board and told myself I had friends over at Troy's.

I had been to the gay center before. In September, I'd gone in to see what gay life was, since I had tried the bars, and they had been so foreign to me. On the bulletin board at the center I had seen a flyer for an event with a long name that included the words Jewish and feminist. I thought, I wonder if those feminists would know any Jewish lesbians? Is there even such a thing as a Jewish lesbian? I decided to go to that seriously named event and corner a Jewish feminist and ask them if they had ever heard of a Jewish lesbian.

That event was at a place called Brooklyn Women's Martial Arts, and it didn't take me long to figure out that New Jewish Agenda Feminist Task Force meant lesbians, a hundred Jewish lesbians on a gym floor. They were singing, "Of all the women who I've loved in my life, it's my grandma Gussie, my father's mom; from Romania she came, Grossman was her name, she was my grandma. . ." I had never even thought of Jewish grandmothers, the Ashkenazi ones like mine, having all come from the same place. To me, Jewish had been a religion, and I had doffed it. Maybe being Jewish was inescapable? This was horrible and exciting all at once. I joined the Task Force, but only for long enough to meet my first Jewish lesbian girlfriend.

I read *Lesbian Nuns: Speaking Out.* I read *Nice Jewish Girls* and *The Tribe of Dina* and Simone de Beauvoir, and I learned to be a radical feminist. I read Audre Lorde, *The Well of Loneliness*, *Rubyfruit Jungle*, and every issue of *Lesbian Connection* that arrived stapled tight to protect reputations. You could get a staple remover as a premium for a multiyear subscription to *LC*.

This was 1987. At work, David the programmer started to get sick. He developed pink patches on his bald head, and no one would touch his keyboard, because there was a rumor he had AIDS. I had read enough pamphlets and gay magazines by then to recognize this as ignorance, fear, and prejudice. But it didn't stop my boss's boss's boss from calling me in for questioning. "Aren't you afraid of getting AIDS?" I'm in a really low risk group. "But from visiting David in the hospital?" You can't get it from touching someone's keyboard or stroking their forehead.

There was ACT-UP then, and blatant homophobia. People were angry in the streets. I went to demonstrations; everybody I knew did. I understood the chutzpa, the humor, and the passion of the Lesbian Avengers motto: "We Recruit." I was giddily out and unapologetically pissed off.

By thirty, I was head over heels into my new world. But you know the riddle about the surgeon's son? A father and son are in a car crash, and the father dies. The son is rushed to the hospital, and they roll him right into surgery. The surgeon looks down at the boy and says, "I can't operate on this boy, he's my son!" How can this be? Turns out the surgeon is the boy's mother, not his father. Even to the most enlightened listener, the person telling the joke almost always has to explain it.

I still fall for that type of thing. Occasionally I come out of the bathroom and catch myself saying the after-the-bathroom prayer. Sometimes when I go to bed, I start saying the before-bedtime prayer. The other day I texted my partner that I feel guilty taking time off to write—"as though I were driving on shabbes." (She, of the Irish upbringing, wrote back, "You love to drive on shabbes!")

Bridging worlds is my heritage. Religion and anti-religion, nationalism and anti-nationalism, conservatism and queerness; shabbes and weekdays, politeness and authenticity, keeping the peace and sticking to your guns. Feminism teaches us suspicion of binaries, but they frame my life. There is a time to plant and a time to uproot, a time to keep silent and a time to speak. There is a time for war and a time for peace.

CHAPTER 2

To Everything a Season

My silences had not protected me. Your silence will not protect you.
—Audre Lorde[1]

The Risks of the Binary

The thesis of this book is that neither strain of conflict engagement, what we've been calling "talking" and "fighting," is essentially good or bad. Certainly, it is better to avoid violence, and talking is a better way for humans to interact than fighting, all things being equal. It is right for all people to consent to the activities in which they participate, and not to be compelled by anyone else to act—again, all things being equal. These are not parenthetical values; they are central to a humane perspective on living. Certainly, when lives are at stake, it is inhumane to hold back for the sake of gentleness.

Clarity about such choices, however, is hard to attain. Most of us pick favorites, identifying more strongly either as talkers or as fighters. We may judge those whose choices don't match our own.

I have had the experience of migrating across cultures, living in communities whose core values differ from one another's to the point of opposition. My stories are all about leaping across social chasms, then building bridges between them, and, again, settling in on one side. I have developed a double affinity for talking and fighting. I am fiercely drawn to both.

Let's examine a colorful Bible rule: "Do not destroy the corners of your beard."[2] The law was understood to prohibit shaving with a straight razor, and it is one reason Jewish men in old pictures have beards. According to the trim-bearded Rabbi Berel Wein, a couple hundred years ago Jewish men first circumvented the prohibition by using "a sulfuric compound that served as a depilatory to remove their facial hair." Better news came with electric shavers, "which allowed one to shave facial hair with a scissors action," providing "the means by which observant Jews could appear as clean-shaven as the rest of American society of the time."[3]

I understand from my siblings and in-laws that the morning electric shaver ritual is not a favorite among well-groomed urban professional American Jewish men. Apparently, it isn't as close a shave as some would prefer. By what happenstance did I learn this? The siblings were talking about their Jewish friend who'd only just learned that he had been adopted as a baby from non-Jewish birth parents and that his ritual conversion to Judaism had been substandard. He was going to be properly converted a week from Tuesday, and, in the meantime, he would be exempt from following much of Jewish law.

By the time I overheard this conversation I'd long been nonobservant, so I pretended to read the paper while my siblings and in-laws weighed in one by one about what law they would most like to be exempt from for a week. "That's easy, I'd eat lobster!" said the foodie. Then one of the men said, "Whoa. I would totally shave with a straight razor."

I've been eliminating the corners of my beard with a straight razor for over twenty-five years. Multiple doctors told me I was endocrine-imbalanced, but that's because they only had two ranges of normal, and I didn't fit either. Chromosomes: x and x. Reproductive utilities: I think we've covered that. Hormones: in some ways like the girl chart, in some ways like the boy chart. They gave me a diagnosis: adrenal cortical hyperplasia. I gave me a gender: butch. It doesn't have as much currency now, but it exists in history, literature, and the culture I came out into. It was exhilarating to claim this name, "butch," because it made it good to be me, a masculine woman by both birth and pleasure; it was edgy and true and recognizable, especially to the lady suitors I was interested in.

Not every matter is a coin with two sides. And not every two-sided coin has a good side and a bad side. We encounter unity as well as complexity, wherein binary is one organizing principle among many for identifying the things, ideas, and people who surround us. We know this, intellectually; it is much harder to live it.

Over and over again in my life I have gravitated toward bridge building, responding to crises and opportunities by convening groups of people to think together, create together, and work together. I was trained to be a negotiator, having studied international conflict and negotiation at the Harvard Kennedy School. I was involved from its start with the Jewish Dialogue Project—an initiative designed to enable Jewish families, schools, and synagogues to heal and build internal relationships despite fiercely held political differences—and I regularly mediate conflict for the clients who seek advice from my colleagues and me at Dragonfly Partners. I routinely form emotional bonds with the executive directors and other leaders with whom I work, counting on trust to keep a channel open for influence and learning. I am as honest and authentic as I can be in these relationships.

At the same time, I am a relentless, dog-with-a-bone fighter. I was raised to believe the world is fundamentally fair, because it was fair—to us. When I became aware of just how unequal a place the world is, and when it became evident to me that the injustices at the foundation of our society would prevail except where some force strong and relentless enough hacks away at them, I became aware of the rightness of fighting.

I imagine that readers who are more familiar with dialogue and negotiation will respond to my descriptions differently than readers with more of a resistance mindset. I get passionate about both approaches to conflict, and I get impatient with both, because, as I've mentioned, I am both peacemaker and provocateur.

Some readers will share this double affinity, drawn to dialogue in some cases and to confrontation in others. As individuals, it is not necessary that we exclusively identify as talkers or fighters. We can engage in different approaches at different times—and, indeed, this book is all about determining what is the right time for each. However, it is very important to recognize our personal biases and dispositions and understand what side of the divide we naturally gravitate toward.

Whatever our individual inclinations, few of us find home in a community of practice that specializes in the combination of dialogue and resistance, because there are few such communities.

Theories have been espoused, papers written, and books published on negotiation methods, mediation styles, and approaches to dialogue. We have books, blogs, and workshops to help us apply these theories to any organizational, civic, or political setting. On the other side of the divide, protest history highlights the philosophical and practical strengths of nonviolent resistance, tested in movements worldwide. Activists and academics have developed critiques and catalogued techniques of labor union–style base building, online campaigning, and the kind of popular mass mobilization we saw in the Civil Rights Movement, the Arab Spring, the Women's March, the Occupy campaign, and the Movement for Black Lives. There are books about armed rebellion and about political tyranny, past, present, and potential. Instead of discussing how to negotiate, they explore how to fight and build power.

Which is better, talking or fighting? I told you I wouldn't say, but where human groups face choices about how to approach powerful opponents within organizations, in communities, or in society, it will serve them well to study four factors that greatly effect these choices: the power dynamics of the conflict, the structural obstacles in the way of certain courses of action, the principles and values to which groups are committed, and the biases and tendencies that prevent them from choosing an approach based on power and principle. If, having done these things, they find that fighting is the best strategy, they should fight. If, instead, they find that negotiation is the best strategy, they have no business doing anything else.

Hawks and Doves

In the early 2000s, a dynamic community organizer named Cody led a workers' rights campaign in Philadelphia, where I now live. Every week, activists converged in the city center with signs demanding sick leave for hundreds of nonunionized workers at a large cultural institution. At first a dozen protesters would show up, but over the course of months demonstrations grew until hundreds gathered each week. The pressure rose, and management got nervous.

At some point during the campaign, I had coffee with Cody, just to catch up. I asked him how he was holding up with the peaking of scale and pressure. He said, "The campaign is going great, but we're facing a problem. Management called. They're freaking out, and they want to meet with us."

"Why is that a problem?" I asked.

Cody answered, "I'm not sure how we should handle that meeting. And I'm not sure what to wear—I don't have a suit." Cody was a sharp dresser, as well as a top-notch campaigner, but he wasn't quite ready to negotiate. I think he would have been happy to grow those protests forever.

The suit was a metaphor, not only for Cody's personal disposition toward conflict but for the institutional biases of the groups he was operating within. These groups were good at organizing and raising a ruckus. They had a detailed repertoire of protest tactics, ranging from leafleting the public through bird-dogging politicians to holding sit-ins in the offices of powerholders. They knew how to agitate against the injustices they faced and how to raise people's expectations so that they would demand something better. They knew how to throw a spotlight on abuses and put their adversaries on the spot. All these things were comfortable and familiar. They knew how to fight—and they knew how to dress for the fight. When you're in the ring, you don't want a suit; you want boxing gloves.

Negotiation was something else entirely. It involved a different set of skills—and a different wardrobe. It took place in a different space, with different norms and customs. All of this could be very disorienting to activists more accustomed to ramping up tension than trying to find common ground.

In the end, Cody made it work. He found his way to the negotiating table with management, they made a deal, and the workers got sick leave. He went on to win many other campaigns with skill and grace and brilliance. Not by himself, of course; Cody worked with amazing comrades whose contributions complemented his. But in social movement spaces, it is the fighting part of the story that gets the snaps, the likes, the retweets, the passion, the pride. I have found little love for dialogue and negotiation in social movement spaces. Activists spend a lot of time thinking about internal processes and how to communicate—but they are much more focused on how they talk to one another than how they engage in dialogue with their opponents.

Just as there are hawks and doves when it comes to military conflict, there are hawks and doves when it comes to social change—those who want to escalate the confrontation and those who want to make a truce. I saw this on one of my return trips to the Middle East. In 2008, I once again traveled to the West Bank, in the Occupied Palestinian Territories, this time with two fellow negotiation trainers. We were hired by Bir Zeit University to conduct a series of workshops on conflict theory and negotiation methods for young Palestinian civil society leaders and senior political leaders, including local activists and officials in the Palestinian Authority. The workshop participants wanted to build their skills for managing disputes across intra-Palestinian political differences, but we also listened to discussions among the young activists and senior leaders as they analyzed the Palestinian-Israeli divide.

There was a universally accepted understanding among the Palestinian participants that Israel's military, economic, political, and geographic positioning gave it more power than the Palestinians. In addition to those obvious measures of power, the Palestinians saw the Israeli decision-making apparatus as singular and sound, as opposed to the diversity of factions who took turns speaking on behalf of Palestinians.

It was my sense that we three trainers agreed with the Palestinians' analysis. Our professional opinions squared with their political ones. We were in sync about the impossibility of negotiations between Israel and the Palestinians at that time, given Israel's powerful military and its relationship with the US. But as trainers, we had chosen to share our negotiation tools with no explicit disclaimer about the potential value of Israeli-Palestinian negotiations.

A few weeks after our trip, the other trainers and I got together to debrief. I said, "We should probe more deeply into what the Palestinians regard as alternatives to negotiation with Israel. I don't think we're useful if we teach negotiation tools in a vacuum. We are teaching that every conflict is negotiable."

One of my colleagues, a long-time negotiation instructor at Harvard Law School, said, "Our expertise lies in what happens until someone decides to leave the negotiating table. Others have expertise in the study of alternatives to negotiation—not us."

Another leading light at Harvard Law, Robert Mnookin, wrote a book a bit like this one, exploring the divide between talking and fighting. He allows that under certain circumstances fighting is the most strategic approach to conflict, the morally required one, or both. But Mnookin's advice is different from mine, because his biases and analysis are different. He falls firmly on the side of the talkers; indeed, he calls himself a negotiation imperialist.

I suspect this clarity of boundaries in the worlds of negotiation theory and training is comprised partly of caution about not feigning expertise where one doesn't have any and partly of fear of the adversarial nature of direct action organizing and movement building and a related fear of violence. It also reflects overconfidence about the proportion of conflicts that can be resolved with no fighting. Just as Cody was far more comfortable on the streets than at the bargaining table, those trained in the arts of negotiation are often ill at ease in protest space. Many have chosen to become negotiators precisely because it fits their aesthetic preferences, social identities, and ideological leanings. They may habitually regard fighters as rude, rash, and unreasonable. They typically perceive negotiation as the rational way to solve problems. As a result, that is their go-to approach, regardless of the circumstances.

We're unlikely to find a group that organizes both cross-community dialogue and mass mobilization. Negotiation and social struggle live in different university departments, different conferences, different journals, and different publishing houses.

When these two realms of practice appear in each other's lexicon, it is typically as a foil. Negotiators deeply value alternatives to negotiation, like organizing or fighting, as conceptual structures for strategy building but rarely as legitimate options for action. As will soon be clear, the core negotiation concept of knowing what to do if negotiation fails sets up the nonnegotiation alternative as something to be avoided.

Similarly, social change organizers like Cody may be intentionally and explicitly fighting for a place at the table, but making reference to dialogue is, in oppositional activist spaces, generally taboo. The brothers Mark and Paul Engler, in their book on mass uprisings, tell a story about an environmental advocacy group whose confrontational approach "pointedly set the group apart from Big Green's dubiously conciliatory operating procedure."[4] In activist circles, the words "dubiously" and "conciliatory" go together as effortlessly as Meghan and Harry.

As we consider the motivations of the talkers and the fighters, we are building a thought bridge for understanding past and present social struggles and internal organizational struggles. This will require readers to notice the specific tendencies each type of changemaker brings to their work. It will also help readers think beyond their own biases and preferences to make more strategic choices.

Habits of Choice

In 1968, when the Black Panther Party was getting off the ground in Seattle, brothers Aaron and Elmer Dixon were among the leaders of its campaign for better schools. At first the Dixons held meetings and sit-ins, using only nonviolent methods of protecting African Americans from racist harassment in the education system. But after Dr. Martin Luther King, Jr. was murdered on April 4, the Seattle Panthers shifted away from nonviolence, says Elmer Dixon, because they no longer believed it was adequate to their gargantuan goal of upending the country's systems of inequality. Such a goal called for armed rebellion. Aaron Dixon remembers saying, "It's time to turn to more violent ways of doing things, because they killed a man of peace through violence. We have no other alternative but to turn towards violence."[5] With all other options exhausted, the Seattle Panthers turned to violence as their last resort.

In 2017, the second biggest soft drink company in the US ran an ad called "Let's Talk." It dramatized a Black Lives Matter protest as a sort of street carnival, out of the middle of which danced celebrity model Kendall Jenner. She grabbed an officer from the police line and jubilantly presented him with a refreshing can of Pepsi. The protest carnival leapt into dance, and the Black Lives Matter marchers celebrated with the cops. In its official statement, PepsiCo said the ad was meant to project "a global message of unity, peace, and understanding."[6] But they pulled the ad off the air after organized pushback from viewers who thought it belittled the newly broadened awareness of the frequency of killings of unarmed Black men by police. Contributing to the backlash was a wry tweet from Bernice King, daughter of Dr. King: "If only Daddy would have known about the power of #Pepsi." Her message: it was hardly time for reconciliation in America.

Pepsi called for dialogue. The Kings chose nonviolent protest. The Panthers moved to armed rebellion. Why did these groups prefer different methods of approaching social struggle?

Social change writers and activists tend to focus on oppositional, unofficial, grassroots political behavior. They may mix it with an understanding of insider, at-the-table political activity, but they rarely give much attention to the study of negotiation and dialogue. Experts on negotiation or organizational dynamics tend toward the opposite, focusing on dialogue, mediation, and other cooperative, if not collaborative, approaches to conflict. They may overlook the fact that to get their needs met, weaker groups usually need to fight first, then negotiate.

When a group picks one method—dialogue or resistance—and sticks with it, its members lose the ability to build power and use it to get what they want. Unions strike to build and consolidate power in order to increase their chances of getting demands met once they do negotiate. Outside of unionized workplaces, groups poised to make change rarely build the skill and habit needed to move through the shifts that justice and peace require in a world of inequity, deprivation, and destruction.

Because of the gap that exists between these two worlds, there is a need for conceptual models that value both approaches and offer insight about when each approach can be effectively deployed. We can develop better strategies for making change if we have a unified framework for disputes inside organizations and communities, in political action, and in social struggle—a single model that brings together conciliatory and antagonistic activities. This book provides that model. It is my intention that we emerge with a useful tool for analyzing historic and contemporary conflicts. We can use this tool to compare, predict, and make our own strategic decisions by accounting for factors that consciously or unintentionally affect the likelihood we will achieve our aims.

Strategic Choice

Progressive media personality Van Jones worked in the Obama White House in 2008 and 2009, where he was, by definition, an insider. That's what "inside" work means—functioning from within the structures of power. Even though he spent years of his life as an "outside" organizer of protest and builder of social movements, Jones chose to serve in government, which meant he followed the policies and practices of the administration and, as a consequence, did a lot of negotiating.

So thoroughly had Jones adapted to inside politics that he blanched when he learned of an online campaign targeting his media nemesis at the time, conservative political commentator Glenn Beck. This wasn't just any activist campaign; it was a boycott led by Color of Change, a resistance organization Jones had helped to create. Beck had called President Obama a racist, and Color of Change was aiming to get him fired from his job at Fox. At first, Jones dismissed the campaign, believing it was futile. In his 2012 political memoir *Rebuild the Dream*, he recalled thinking it was better to ignore Beck and his ilk, reflecting that "life in the White House requires a thick skin, and a laser-like focus on the task at hand."

Meanwhile Jones's cofounder at Color of Change, James Rucker, was responding to skepticism about the campaign from non-Fox journalists. Rucker later wrote that many media outlets had "succumbed to the lazy conventional wisdom that our campaign could not generate the financial pressure necessary to dislodge Beck."[7] Jones also told Rucker that a boycott would only get Beck more wound up, and he was right. Shifting the media spotlight away from his own sins, Beck and his supporters targeted none other than Jones himself, discrediting him for the far-left politics that had characterized his twenties. Jones decided to fold, quitting his White House job to keep from being a problem for the Obama administration.

From his reclaimed vantage point outside the White House, Jones reflected on this inside-outside dynamic. He thought about how few

progressives protested even the most centrist of President Obama's policies and how they had allowed the newly formed Tea Party to push deeply
conservative views into America's political mainstream. In so doing, he
argued, progressives had "overestimated our achievement in 2008" and
"underestimated our opponent in 2009."

"Too many of us sat down at the very moment when we should have
stood up," Jones reflected. The movement-building momentum that had
gotten Obama elected was over. Progressives "were in the suites when we
should have been in the streets. Many repositioned our grassroots organizations to be at the table in order to work with the administration." Instead,
he concluded, fighting for the people requires "a willingness to walk with
the White House when possible—and to walk boldly ahead of that same
White House, when necessary."[8]

Underscoring Jones's conclusion, Color of Change, with dozens of
coalition members and the tens of thousands of individuals they had
mobilized, won their campaign and pushed Beck off Fox for good.

Group tendencies toward dialogue or peaceful protest or disobedi-
ent protest are common. Each time a group gets what it wants through its
preferred approach, that approach is validated, and any tendency by that
group to practice another approach is diminished.

Yet consistently choosing one approach to conflict and change limits
the ability of a group to get where it is headed. Cody needed to work hard
to get from fighting to talking; it wasn't natural for him. Pepsi tripped over
itself rushing to talk about race. Regardless of the source of those tendencies—whether individual influences like social pressure, desire to belong,
ego, emotion, habit, or institutional traits, including strategic preferences,
moral principles, or real-world limits on choice of action—being perma-
nently stuck in talking or fighting mode limits a group's chances of getting
what it wants.

Groups with their eyes focused on their goals move lithely from one
strategy to another, like Cody ultimately did, choosing a path that is both
in line with their principles and propels them toward those goals.

What Makes Hawks Hawks and Doves Doves

As we work for change, our beliefs, habits, identities, and experiences may
stand in for a strategy to get us what we're fighting for. The members of
any given group have conflict styles as diverse as their individual combi-
nations of personality traits, racial and gender identities and experiences,

cultural, socioeconomic and educational backgrounds, mental health histories, relationship stories, and beliefs—including beliefs about how change itself happens.

Imagine you are in eighth grade. You're thirteen years old, and English is your favorite class. Mr. Rush has just asked the student in front of you, Erica, to distribute blank writing journals to everyone in the classroom.

Erica hands out the blank notebooks, starting at the far end of the room, aiming to get to her own seat last. By the time Erica gets to you, she's only got one book left. She holds it in her hand, avoids eye contact with you, and looks over at Mr. Rush. "There's only one left, Mr. Rush, and two of us still don't have one."

You say, "You know how much I love writing, Mr. Rush."

Erica says to you, "That is totally unfair. You are being so mean." To Mr. Rush, Erica says, "I should be the one that gets this book. I passed them out, after all!"

If that were really you back in that classroom, what do think you would do?

As individuals, we choose how to approach conflict with a combination of conscious choice and personal predispositions toward one approach or another. Our styles are influenced by events earlier even than eighth grade. Kenneth W. Thomas and Ralph H. Kilmann, authors of a widely studied conflict typology, found that individual conflict style is made up of "personal beliefs, values, and motives that 'push' one's conflict behavior in a consistent direction."[9] We may find ourselves reflected in one of the five conflict styles identified in the Thomas-Kilmann Conflict Styles grid (see Figure 2.1): collaborating, accommodating, competing, avoiding, and compromising.

If you tend toward competing, you might insist that Erica give you the book, or you might make a reasoned case for why it should be yours—or you might just grab it. An accommodator would let Erica keep it. An avoider might leave it to Erica and Mr. Rush to decide.

If your style is compromising, you might suggest to Erica that you share the notebook, maybe by taking turns using it. If your style is collaborating, you would attempt to work it out together. You might say, "I really want it, but I know you do too. How can we figure this out? Any extra books somewhere? Mr. Rush? What do you guys think?" Maybe everyone in the class could contribute a quarter and pay for the extra notebook.

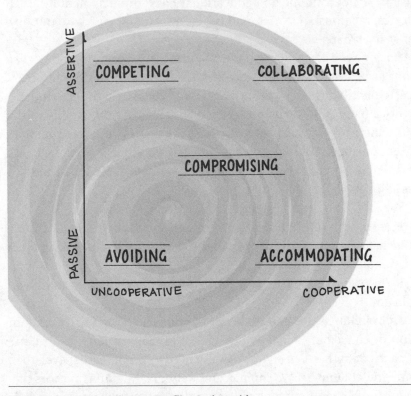

Figure 2.1: Thomas-Kilmann Conflict Styles grid
© *Kenneth Thomas and Ralph Kilmann. Graphic by Rosi Greenberg.*

You can see that each of the conflict styles reflects a convergence of two dimensions of our psychology: cooperativeness and assertiveness. If you're very assertive but not so cooperative, you'll hold onto the book, even though it will anger Erica, and she won't have one. If you rank high on cooperative but low on assertive, you'll be more likely to let her keep it.

Conveniently, personality psychology's list of primary traits also has a count of five: extroversion, openness to experience, agreeableness, conscientiousness, and neuroticism. The psychologists say that these personality traits are products of socioeconomic background, birth order, early development, physical and mental health, relationship history, education, gender experience, and many other factors.[10]

Psychologists who study how personality influences behavior have found that each of the five primary personality traits seems to correspond to one of the five conflict styles. People whose most prominent personality trait is extroversion tend to have a collaborative or competitive conflict style and rarely an avoiding style. People with strong tendencies toward conscientiousness or openness typically have a collaborative conflict style. People who are agreeable tend toward collaborative and avoiding styles, and those with a dominant personality trait of neuroticism also tend toward an avoiding conflict style.[11]

What happens when you create a motley mix of people with this range of personality traits, life experience, ideological commitments, habits, and skill sets? What happens when teams of workers, neighbors, or groups of citizens show up to a conflict with a combination of conscious choices and predispositions toward one approach or another?

Groups also develop characteristic styles of approaching conflict. As a group develops over time, it is influenced by the conflict styles of its members, along with their demographic mix, political diversity, personalities, skills, training, and experiences. But the group's style is influenced by its characteristics as a *group* as well—its internal dynamics and cultural norms, its external collaborators and detractors, events and changes in the world around it, and the accumulated history of the group's past responses to conflict.

Group Approaches to Conflict

In our workplaces, we may find colleagues forming competitive factions around an issue, poised for fights with each other and with management. At the same time, others may be trying to engage in dialogue with those they oppose.

Throughout the 2010s, for example, our team at Dragonfly Partners worked with dozens of progressive nonprofit organizations and other activist groups riven by the urgency of confronting racism inside the organization and in the work itself. Director after director would describe racially diverse groups of disgruntled millennials organizing against them in their own workplaces. As they explained their dilemma, the director would invariably add that a separate set of staff had voluntarily joined a new diversity committee set up by Human Resources and seemed eager to be cooperative contributors. "Why," they would ask, "won't the disgruntled millennials just join the diversity committee?"

The directors recognized that the diversity committee was formed by workers who believed they could get what they wanted through dialogue. What they did not recognize was that the workers who organized against management may have wanted many of the same changes as the committee members, but they believed that achieving these changes would require a fight.

The same pattern is apparent when one group of activists is marching in the streets to demand new legislation, while another group works directly with elected officials to change the same law. The same dynamic is at play when some environmental groups cooperate with big business and others refuse to. There is a vibrant Black Caucus within the US Congress, yet some activists in the Movement for Black Lives believe our electoral system is rigged against them and unworthy of their participation.

We encounter groups with divergent strategies but shared goals failing to communicate—let alone coordinate their strategies.

A convenient way to contrast talkers and fighters is to consider the range of groups in the twenty-first-century US working to turn this country around, focusing first on those solidly in the resistance camp, and then on those who champion bridge building.

In This Corner, the Resistance

Readers more at home in the world of social movements share the tagline "Resist." You saw it on the backs of cars whose drivers hated Trump. These are people who choose loyalty to an identity or community of resistance; they are most at home among people who want to fight. To many in this group, the only appropriate response to the world is resistance, until all people are free.

"Resist" is a pronouncement aimed at potential recruits that says there's no time for the inside game, because the power difference between those calling for change and those with the keys to the change is too great. This power difference is systemic and endemic; it is built in. It requires entrenchment in a long, deep project of upending the system. Until Dr. King's giant triplets of racism, materialism, and militarism, along with the other begats of white supremacy and capitalism, give way to a world centered on the equality and well-being of all people, this group's mode is resistance. Until patriarchy too has finished its work of poisoning men and ruining the lives of women and gender-nonconforming people, resistance is the daily way. Inch by inch in calm times, and in bursts when public crises open the conversation wide, a fighting posture is required to flip the inequalities built into our economy, our schools, our cultures, and our mindsets. Systemic inequality requires ongoing resistance.

To the Resistance, we need big changes to society, whether that means ending the extreme and growing wealth gap, shifting from a military-dependent economy, repairing centuries of economic domination by white people over African Americans, or the equal participation of people other than men at all levels of government. We need to end corporate greed and build communities where immigrants and people from all racial and economic backgrounds belong. We need an equalizing of opportunity and reward for people of all gender identities and expressions and with every type of relationship with the criminal justice system.

For many who choose resistance, it is not only time to build power to win campaigns and change legislation. It is time to penetrate and fully overhaul, in many cases even overturn, the very systems that have failed us. It's time for a new social contract that neutralizes the roots of injustice.

And in This Corner, the Bridge Builders

Since big change is rarely achieved through a homogeneous string of acts of resistance, experienced resisters recognize and seize the moments when they have succeeded in securing a space at the negotiating table, but, nonetheless, we would be less surprised to find people who work in community dialogue, alternative dispute resolution, or person-to-person advocacy within the context of our legislative and electoral processes sitting comfortably with their opponents. They too may seek big changes in society, including racial and economic equality, a sustainable climate, peaceful international relations, and justice for immigrants, LGBTQI people, women, and people with disabilities. Their estimation or inclination is that they will collect more flies with honey than with vinegar, or that dialogue and conciliation are the more humane approach to conflict and change.

When President Barack Obama said in his 2008 victory speech, "I will listen to you, especially when we disagree," I fell more deeply in love with him than I'd been. Sitting in our living room listening to him speaking to the crowds in Chicago's Grant Park that night, I felt moved, and I texted that line straight out to my besties.

That was a moment for me, because before John Edwards's exit from the presidential nomination race the previous January, I had been influenced by Edwards's criticisms of Obama's naiveté about overcoming disagreement through listening. After all, it was a mystery how to apply a listening strategy on the scale of a third-of-a-billion-strong country. It was as much of a mystery how to apply the listening approach to negotiations with the pharmaceutical and health insurance industries.

Edwards made me doubt Obama's approach. He said, "Some people argue that we're going to sit at a table with these people and they're going to voluntarily give their power away. I think it is a complete fantasy; it will never happen."[12] Nobel Prize–winning economist Paul Krugman reflected on this public debate, saying Edwards's comments were "pretty clearly a swipe at Mr. Obama, who has repeatedly said that health reform should be negotiated at a 'big table' that would include insurance companies and drug companies." Obama weighed in again: "We want to reduce the power of drug companies and insurance companies and so forth, but the notion that they will have no say-so at all in anything is just not realistic."

Krugman backed Edwards:

> It's actually Mr. Obama who's being unrealistic here, believing that the insurance and drug industries—which are, in large part, the cause of our health care problems—will be willing to play a constructive role in health reform. The fact is that there's no way to reduce the gross wastefulness of our health system without also reducing the profits of the industries that generate the waste.
>
> As a result, drug and insurance companies—backed by the conservative movement as a whole—will be implacably opposed to any significant reforms. And what would Mr. Obama do then? . . . Anyone who thinks that the next president can achieve real change without bitter confrontation is living in a fantasy world. . . . Nothing Mr. Obama has said suggests that he appreciates the bitterness of the battles he will have to fight if he does become president, and tries to get anything done.[13]

A lot of people defended Obama against Krugman and Edwards. Here's how one blogger described Edwards's approach in that primary season:

> Regardless of the issue or opponent, Edwards has the same policy prescription: fight. The former trial lawyer's reading of his own biography is formed by conflict, a natural career arc from the schoolyard to the courtroom, and suggests that as president he would remain a scrapper.
>
> "You've got to send somebody into the arena who's ready for the fight," said Edwards, pointing to his stomach to say he has the fight

"in here"—an implied contrast with Obama, whom he portrays as too "analytical" to bring about change.[14]

Obama brought us the Affordable Care Act, but we don't know what more we could have gotten had he kept the pharmaceutical and insurance companies out of the early stages of policy development.

It is instructive to examine the fighting and talking threads in a single changemaking story. Sometimes these are two competing threads, as they are in the health care debate between Edwards and Obama. Sometimes we can find the fighting and talking threads woven around each other in a single coherent strategy. Were we to go in search of groups that optimize their use of both talking and fighting, we would bump right into a labor union. If you or a family member have been in a union, or if you've ever watched *Norma Rae*, you know that labor-management relations are all about the dance between negotiation and one-sided action. The union grows its membership. At first, management refuses to enter negotiations for pay raises or better working conditions. The union calls a strike to demonstrate power. The two sides talk, they cut a deal, and the workers vote to ratify a new contract. Unions give us the perfect example of negotiation and fighting as two steps of a single dance.

Labor Unions: Negotiation among Enemies

In the US, workers have been organizing themselves into unions to negotiate for better pay and working conditions since the late 1800s. From its all-time high in the 1950's, union membership has declined in this century, with the fast-tracking of union-bashing laws in statehouses across the country. Yet, today, where unions are strong, the power of the workers is a formidable changemaking force, and it features a nimble back-and-forth between organizing the workers, threatening and sometimes mobilizing a strike or other labor action, and, of course, negotiation.

In this lively 2019 confrontation between management and workers, John Samuelson, president of the Transit Workers Union International, spared no venom in telling the president of American Airlines that AA's mechanics refused to give up their benefits:

> I stand here to tell you in front of this whole room, in front of everybody, anybody who's listening, that you're not gonna get what you want. And if this erupts into the bloodiest, ugliest battle that

the United States labor movement ever saw, that's what's gonna happen.

You're already profitable enough. You compare your profit level to United; you compare it to Delta; start thinking about your own work force. Don't think about where you're at in terms of profitability relative to other airlines in the industry. Three billion bucks and you're looking for more concessions, and these concessions are off of our backs. That's simply not happening.

And you said a very interesting point before about mediation, negotiation, [but] perhaps we'll get to a point where there's [unilateral terms set by management]—and I'll leave you with this . . . [i]f we ever get to [that] point, we are gonna engage in absolutely vicious strike action against American Airlines, the likes of which you've never seen. Not organized by airline people but organized by a guy that came out of the New York City subway system, that's well-inclined to strike power and who understands that the only way to challenge power is to aggressively take it to them.[15]

It was not a loving exchange, but Samuelson does a whizbang job of highlighting the best of what talk and action can do when they're part of a unified strategy. Among unions there is a range of sociopolitical orientations; not all unions are trying to change the social and economic relations of the country. But their theories of change share the doctrine that workers united have power; that the power of the united workers, aka the power of the union when exercised against management, can yield gains for the workers; that the union can calibrate the increased power needed to win at the bargaining table; and that, like a bellows, building power and bargaining are the inhale and the exhale of a group facing power and in search of change.

Fighting to Get to the Table

Before we associate fighting narrowly with strikers and protesters, let's think of it more broadly as unilateral action—action a group takes on its own or in coalition with other groups facing the same powerful opponent. Unilateral action is the natural territory of unions seeking a better deal for workers. It is obviously home base for police forces and armies, lawyers, and competitive businesspeople. Think about it: it is also the realm of terrorists and freedom fighters throughout history.

That's intuitive, but it may be novel to think of all these fighters in a single category.

Unilateral action can be the territory of disgruntled workers in a nonunion setting, whether in a sweatshop, in a nonprofit organization, or at McDonald's. And, of course, it is home base for activists protesting politicians who don't fulfill campaign promises, organizers who pressure manufacturers to end human rights abuses, climate campaigners who want to turn big oil on its head, and socialists who want to raise inheritance taxes to 100 percent.

Negotiators can also benefit from a nontheoretical relationship with one-sided tactics, because sometimes the other side has too much power for the negotiator to get what they need. The most honored of negotiators say as much: "Negotiations under conditions of asymmetry . . . are a paradox," wrote the international conflict theorist William Zartman. Equality is a prerequisite for negotiation.[16] A weaker group is best off fighting to equalize power before entering a negotiation, or it will have trouble reaching a deal that sticks. In practice, Nelson Mandela observed the same: "Only free men can negotiate; prisoners can't enter in contracts."[17]

A negotiator's bias in favor of deal-making can prevent us from noticing that power dynamics sometimes render negotiation useless—or dangerous. Negotiators put themselves at risk if they think unilateral action belongs only to angry protesters, disgruntled workers, cutthroat politicians, ruthless lawyers, and generals. Think about it; no humane approach to negotiation would propose that David negotiate with Goliath.

In his famous 1963 "Letter from a Birmingham Jail," Dr. King exposed this disconnect:

> I have almost reached the regrettable conclusion that the Negro's great stumbling block in the stride toward freedom is not the White Citizen's Counciler [sic] or the Ku Klux Klanner, but the white moderate who is more devoted to "order" than to justice; who prefers a negative peace which is the absence of tension to a positive peace which is the presence of justice; who constantly says "I agree with you in the goal you seek, but I can't agree with your methods of direct action;" who paternalistically feels he can set the timetable for another man's freedom; who lives by the myth of time and who constantly advises the Negro to wait until a "more convenient season."[18]

There is a time for power building and a time for problem solving. We can understand and strategize conflict behavior more effectively if we understand these as organically connected through the unified framework introduced in the next chapter, a framework that accounts for both power and principle.

CHAPTER 3

Yes, No, or Never: When Do We Fight?

Remember Cody, who led the campaign for sick pay? Remember how he didn't have a suit to wear to meet with the boss? Of course, he didn't really need a suit. Nelson Mandela didn't wear a suit for tea with the Queen of England. What Cody didn't have was experience getting this far in a power-building project, or, more likely, he liked being out in the streets and felt that talking with the very target of his campaign—management—was not an organizer's job. Whatever your "suit" is, if you don't have one hanging in the back of the closet, you aren't fighting to win. You're fighting to fight.

At the other end of the spectrum, when it becomes clear that decision makers will not respond to persuasion, it becomes necessary to act without their consent. It is time to fight—that is, to take unilateral action to build power. Frederick Douglass spelled out this philosophy of resistance:

> The whole history of the progress of human liberty shows that all concessions yet made to her august claims have been born of earnest struggle. The conflict has been exciting, agitating, all-absorbing, and for the time being, putting all other tumults to silence. It must do this or it does nothing. If there is no struggle there is no progress.
>
> This struggle may be a moral one, or it may be a physical one, and it may be both moral and physical, but it must be a struggle. Power concedes nothing without a demand. It never did and it never will. Find out just what any people will quietly submit to and you have found out the exact measure of injustice and wrong which will be imposed upon them, and these will continue till they are resisted with either words or blows, or with both.[1]

In chapter 2 we explored two approaches to conflict. Sometimes the best approach to change is dialogue, and sometimes it is resistance. Each is the right choice under certain conditions. The stakes are high.

A Time to Talk and a Time to Fight

We've been focused on the dynamic between the two strategic approaches to conflict. The first, which until now we have called dialogue, negotiation, or talking, includes activities taken on with the consent of both (or all) parties to the conflict. The second approach, which until now we've called resistance, protest, or fighting, includes activities taken on unilaterally by one group against a second group, without the consent of that second group.

Let's imagine that all the activities and methods of social conflict and struggle are lined up in two columns. Methods of dialogue, negotiation, and talking are lined up in Column A, and methods of resistance, protest, and fighting are lined up in Column B.

Column A activity is consensual. Its purpose is to resolve the issues at the heart of the struggle. Column A methods are attempts at joint problem solving among the parties to the conflict.

Negotiation, mediation, and voting are methods of consensual problem solving. Everyone who participates in a negotiation or subjects themselves to mediation or goes to the ballot box to vote is participating in a process of decision-making (or a sort of problem resolution) by choice. These are all examples of a Column A approach to conflict. Obviously, Column A isn't only about friendly conversations! It includes any type of problem solving that happens within a system that everyone involved in the conflict has signed up for. This includes a public dialogue on how a school system should spend its money, a summit between the presidents of the US and Russia, or even binding arbitration among neighbors fighting over a property boundary. It includes a corporate shareholders' meeting, a conversation between an elected representative and a citizen lobbyist, and a candidate collecting the signatures needed to qualify for a place on the ballot. It includes electoral contests where two opponents are actively slandering and denouncing one another—yet each agrees to abide by the outcome determined by voters on election day.

While Column A methods are consensual, the methods in Column B are chosen and enacted unilaterally by one party to the conflict against another (or others). You don't ask the target of your protest whether they want you to picket in front of their shop. When you organize a demon-stration outside a public dialogue on school funding or stage an inter-ruption at a corporate shareholders' meeting, your action is in Column B. When the president of one country tweets a threat to the president of another, that's Column B, unless the two of them have a secret strategy of which the threat is a part. Whereas participating in a town hall called by your representative is a Column A activity, disrupting the town hall is in Column B, since your action is outside the consensual town hall process. A workers' or students' strike, walkout, or sick-out is a power-building Column B action.

The power-building methods in Column B include demands expressed through public education, rallies, marches, petitions, boycotts, sit-ins, street theater, and other acts of civil disobedience. The nonviolence theo-rist Gene Sharp categorized all of these methods and more into buckets: protest; persuasion of other potential protesters; social, economic, and political noncooperation; nonviolent intervention. Nonviolent interven-tion includes hunger striking, nonviolent occupation, and the creation of alternative social, economic, and political structures parallel to those authorized by the group's opponents.[2] Activists and scholars continue to expand and update Sharp's catalogue, but his assertion that nonconsen-sual action is a key to building power is key to understanding Column B.

The community member who organizes neighbors in support of a property boundary dispute, circulates an online petition against a piece of bad legislation, or invites new people to join their activist group is using the power-building methods of Column B. This is friendly activity, and it doesn't directly involve the target of the campaigns, but it is a step in building the power of one side against the other. Not only is disrupting a corporate shareholder meeting a Column B activity, so is organizing activ-ists to participate in the disruption. When citizens publicly shame their representatives, divest from corporations with egregious human rights practices, or write letters to the editor making demands of City Council, they are engaging in the methods of Column B, methods whose purpose is to build the power of their position.

Nonviolent methods are not the only way to build power. For starters, one person's nonviolence is another person's terror: a disciplined nonvio-lent street blockade preventing entrance to a bank accused of predatory practices will predictably be experienced by some passersby as violent. In subsequent chapters we will also consider groups whose protest repertoire includes intentionally damaging public or private property. And, of course, some weaker groups take up arms to build their power.

Governments use police and military violence, though this is frequently in the exercise of the power the state already has rather than to build up the state's power. More on that shortly. Whether we call them terrorists or freedom fighters, non-state groups have at times chosen violent methods as the cornerstone of a power-building strategy. Historical examples tumble in once you start thinking about it: the Irish Republican Army, the Jewish resistance in Nazi-occupied Poland, the Algerian resistance to French rule, Al-Qaeda, and so on. These groups targeted the power of states, just as so many countries were formed when revolutionary groups used armed struggle to grow their power against the governments they sought to topple.

It isn't surprising, then, that we can list groups whose fights for domestic social change have incorporated armed resistance into their strategies or have not hesitated to prepare themselves for armed self-defense against state violence. Before the Civil War, Black preacher Nat Turner and white abolitionist John Brown each used violence in their fight to end slavery; key to both their strategies was organizing their comrades to steal weapons from slaveowners and from the government. In the 1970s, the Weather Underground fought to undermine institutionalized white supremacy by bombing corporate and government buildings, and the Black Liberation Army organized revolutionary violence to counter the violence of police forces that targeted Black communities.[3]

Whether armed or nonviolent, what is the purpose of this unilateral nonconsensual action? It is to build power, not to resolve the demand that a group is protesting about.

Resistance is expensive; people get hurt. The costs include strained relationships, time and money, and the opportunity cost of resources made unavailable for other political causes, to feed people, and for pleasure. It may mean intentionally risking arrest or being subject to police or military violence. The reward of resistance isn't getting what you're fighting for, not quite yet. The reward of resistance is power—power to go another round and, if necessary, another— power to grow the movement for the long haul.

The reward, at some point, is also the power to negotiate a satisfying deal—if not a forever deal, at least one to set the foundation for another bout in Column B.

If one party is much stronger, the weaker group will need to become more powerful. Whether by violent force or through nonviolent action, Column B activity will restore sufficient balance that negotiation will become viable. Power is built in Column B and embodied in Column A. Figure 3.1 demonstrates this dynamic.

Consider the cause of gay rights in the US, which manifested for years as a protest movement. After decades of building power through organizing, campaigning, and mass mobilization—all Column B activities—activists could make gains through Column A methods, such as achieving legislative wins and working with corporate management to establish inclusive workplace policies.

Let's step into an imaginary example. You work in the cramped, twelve-person office of a company that sells safety goggles. The newest member of the staff is Lacey, who came in last winter and shares a cubicle with you. Last week, you and Lacey began to smell cigarette smoke coming through the office ventilation system, and it hasn't stopped. The smoke aggravates your asthma. But the boss has never been responsive to the needs of the staff, and you don't want to ruffle feathers, so you say nothing.

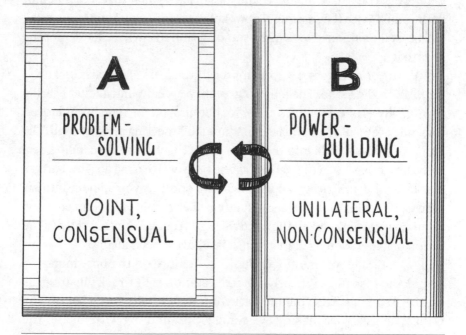

Figure 3.1: Columns A and B: two approaches to conflict

Lacey is only somewhat annoyed by the smoke itself, but they are enraged by your reluctance to go to bat for your own health. You know that going to the boss won't help. You tell Lacey why you are hesitant.[4]

While it is true that you don't have enough power to get your needs met through negotiation, it is true only in the present. You recognize that you can probably find a way to dramatize your case and get the boss's attention. If you choose not to, your asthma will get worse. You have a choice to make, and, in the end, you choose your health.

You and Lacey hatch a plan. The two of you will go right to the boss, in the hope that the recent spike in goggles sales has put him in a generous mood. If he fails to act, you will wrangle the other nine employees to sign a letter demanding the boss do something about the smoke. If he doesn't respond to that, you'll hold a meeting during lunchtime to strategize with fellow staff members.

Your plan begins in Column A. After all, this may not even be a conflict; you may not have faith in the boss, but Lacey does, so you cover your bases. Worst case, the boss doesn't address the problem, and you're on to Column B to build the power of your cause. If your first pressure tactic, the letter, fails, you'll have mobilized the staff to back your cause; that's money in the bank! With the newfound power of a group backing your cause, you will be well-positioned to take the sort of action that will be harder for the boss to ignore.

With your strategy set, you approach the boss. The sales spike did nothing for his mood. The following week, you hand him a letter bearing the signatures of everyone in the office but him, but he remains unmoved. You and Lacey call an unofficial lunchtime staff meeting at Kelly's Deli. The group decides to walk into the boss's office together to demand he deal with the smoke. Everyone gathers in the hallway wearing goggles and gas masks waiting for Lacey to open the boss's door. As you all pour into his office, he lifts his voice in rage, shouting, "Leave this office immediately! What do you think this is, the circus?!" Liza from accounting catches the action on video, and by dinner time it is all over social media.

As your support multiplies and the pressure on the boss increases, he hides in his office. When a local radio station calls to ask him to speak on the issue, he calls you and Lacey in. "Alright already, what do you want?" he asks, not making eye contact and fiddling with his tie. You have returned to Column A. This is not a friendly conversation, but it is a consensual one: you are all in the room by choice, you are solving the cigarette smoke problem, and everyone is participating in the problem-solving process.

There are good reasons employees may be reluctant to go to Column B against their bosses. Bosses have the power not only to ignore staff concerns but also to delay a raise, cancel a promotion, and, in most states, fire people they don't like. A boss is also a human being with a face and a heart and loved ones in their life, and a worker may be reluctant to fight with someone for whom they have empathy. Some workers may want to avoid fighting because of a belief or a sense that even a highly reluctant boss will eventually hear the staff's concerns.

We may succeed in changing minds by appealing to the reason and morality of decision makers. One hundred years after Douglass's speech about power and struggle, Dr. King wrote, "Lamentably, it is an historical fact that privileged groups seldom give up their privileges voluntarily. Individuals may see the moral light and voluntarily give up their unjust posture; but . . . groups tend to be more immoral than individuals."[5] A boss is a person, and sometimes even a very powerful person can be influenced by a weaker group. But with so many other factors influencing them, it may still become necessary to compel a leader through antagonistic action. When a weaker group faces not an individual but a group or an institution, the weaker group will always need to go to Column B to be taken seriously.

Groups move from Column A to Column B as necessary to build power, and from Column B back to Column A when power is sufficiently equalized to facilitate an acceptable negotiation outcome. A group may go through a sequence of joint problem-solving and power-building activities as strategy indicates, or they may engage in joint problem-solving activities and power-building activities simultaneously. (If you like flow charts, you can follow this process in Figure 3.2.)

Taking Sides

Within a community, an organization, or a social movement, we can expect to find individuals and groups with specialized interest or expertise in either negotiation or protest or in any of the many methods within each of the two approaches to conflict. Because of the range of expertise, experience, philosophical commitments, constraints, preferences, biases, and other influences on people working toward a common goal, there is frequently a range of approaches and methods championed within the community, organization, or social movement.

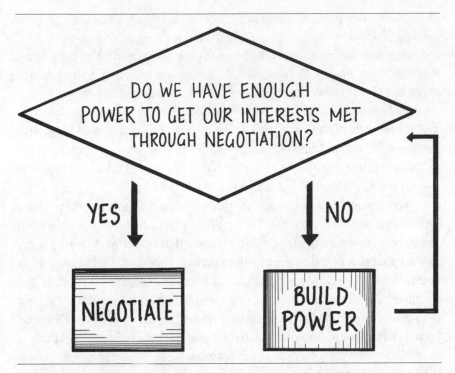

Figure 3.2: The power-building cycle

At best, this diversity of approaches can be coordinated and, at least, conducted with supportive cooperation. Ideally, we would all be able to get along, even if our chosen approaches and methods are different. Unfortunately, it usually doesn't work out that way. More typically, commitment to one approach or another leads to rifts and factionalization in neighborhoods, organizations, coalitions, or movements. It may even prevent groups with shared goals from maintaining channels of communication.

During the 1950s and 1960s, some civil rights groups were committed to changing laws by working inside the electoral and legislative systems. They backed sympathetic candidates and built relationships with high-ranking political leaders and other powerful influencers. Other civil rights groups focused on outsider action, whether through door-to-door organizing, lunch counter sit-ins, or armed resistance; these power-building activities were the center of Black liberation action for years. The insider negotiators and the outsider activists were deeply critical of each other's approaches, and there were fierce struggles between proponents of dialogue and advocates of power building.[6]

Not only do fighters frequently consider talkers to be sellouts; they tend to relate to talkers in the spirit of their approach of choice—fighting. But talkers can also create discord in a group. Many who prefer consensual Column A methods when facing their actual opponents nevertheless fall into Column B activities when conflict arises within their own group. You may have experienced such a switch yourself. This struggle inside a faction, an organization, a social movement, or a political group leads to familiar intragroup dynamics, with our approach biases playing out internally in ways that mirror our approaches to struggle with outside forces.

Intergroup struggle over approaches to changemaking is beautifully illustrated by Dr. King's dispute with a group of eight white Alabama clergymen. These seven Christians and a Jew had been among the signatories of an "Appeal for Law and Order and Common Sense." Then, in April 1963, they published a statement opposing the nonviolent campaign being planned for Birmingham, Alabama, to target segregation in employment, public facilities, shops, and schools. The campaign had other prominent civil rights leaders at the helm, including the Birmingham-based Reverend Fred Shuttlesworth, but the white clergy admonished Dr. King personally. They wrote: "We . . . strongly urge our own Negro community to withdraw support from these demonstrations, and to unite locally in working peacefully for a better Birmingham. When rights are consistently denied, a cause should be pressed in the courts and in negotiations among local leaders, and not in the streets. We appeal to both our white and Negro citizenry to observe the principles of law and order and common sense."[7]

Stick to Column A, they admonished. Column B methods are immoral.

Dr. King's response was his "Letter from a Birmingham Jail," in which he described the relationship between joint and unilateral problem solving. In explaining his embrace of direct action organizing and civil disobedience, Dr. King wrote:

> You may well ask: "Why direct action? Why sit ins, marches and so forth? Isn't negotiation a better path?" You are quite right in calling for negotiation. Indeed, this is the very purpose of direct action. Nonviolent direct action seeks to create such a crisis and foster such a tension that a community which has constantly refused to negotiate is forced to confront the issue. It seeks so to dramatize the issue that it can no longer be ignored. My citing the creation of tension as part of the work of the nonviolent resister may sound

rather shocking. But I must confess that I am not afraid of the word "tension" . . . the kind of tension in society that will help men rise from the dark depths of prejudice and racism to the majestic heights of understanding and brotherhood. The purpose of our direct action program is to create a situation so crisis packed that it will inevitably open the door to negotiation.[8]

To Dr. King, taking action in Column B was not immoral. To the contrary, it was morally essential to know when it was time to take unilateral power-building action, but to do so only to return to negotiation.

Some activists personally identify as protesters, resisters, and outsiders. For this group, Column B is a natural location; we can say they have a Column B bias. Those not accustomed to protest may dismiss outsider activists as fringe weaklings wasting their time with silly signs or troublemakers violating laws for their own glory. We can say that those observers have a bias toward Column A—toward dialogue and against controversy. They, in turn, are missing the power of organizing, which in many cases is the only strategy that can bring about a win.

The strategy that effective groups use for changing the decisions of the powerful is to balance problem-solving activity and power-building action in a strategic sequence. The dance between Column A and Column B activities is at the center of social-change strategy.

Column C: Vanquishing

There is a third ring in this circus of approaches to conflict. If your group is weaker than the other party to the conflict, you might ask, "Can my opponent become a viable negotiation partner? Could they at any point be positioned to work out a deal with us?" If the answer is no, there would be no point in building power for the purpose of negotiation. You might not have to ask; you might know intuitively that negotiation is morally or practically inconceivable in a given situation. When the group or person holding the reins—Hitler, Stalin, Trump, corporate conglomerates—is so ruthless, so empty of the ability or desire ever to agree to the authority of a court of law or a mediated conversation, Column A is a pipe dream, but so is Column B. (See Figure 3.3.)

In this scenario, even if we had enough power to get to the bargaining table, we wouldn't bargain with the more powerful group. In this instance, we don't want those in power to meet our demands; rather, we want their power to be neutralized, destroyed. This is when we want to vanquish the other and overthrow the system, turn the order of things upside-down. It is where killing and war become imaginable, or even appealing, to groups with less power. With or without imagining violence, we imagine some version of revolution.

When the weaker party to a conflict takes Column C action, they are rebels seeking to neutralize the power of a stronger group. This story of vanquishing can be liberatory, but there is a flip side to Column C; vanquishing can be destructive, and in the wrong hands it is tyranny. Thoroughly vanquishing the power of the other is the modus operandi of tyrants. Whereas revolution is the method of the weak to vanquish the powerful, tyranny is the method of the powerful to squash the weak. Vanquishing is complex; it may challenge our notions of good and bad.

Let's step outside the realm of social conflict to consider an example of vanquishing in the context of international relations. In 2011, Libyan leader Colonel Muammar el-Gaddafi was engaged in a ruthless civil war against his own civilian population. Across the world, people and governments were enraged, and the UN passed Security Council Resolution 1973 calling for military action in Libya.

The intention expressed in UNSCR 1973 was to put an end to Gaddafi's harming of civilians and achieve a ceasefire. The resolution demanded his compliance, authorized member states to trespass on Libya's sovereignty, established a no-fly zone, enforced an arms embargo, banned Libya from flying its own planes, and froze the assets of its leaders.

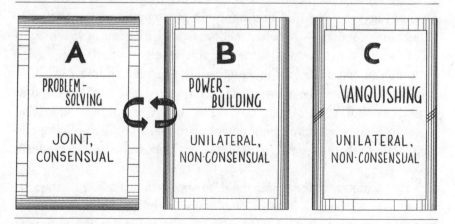

Figure 3.3: Columns A-B-C: three approaches to conflict

In the guise of enacting the Security Council resolution, NATO and the Arab League sent military forces to protect Libyan rebels who were resisting Gaddafi's aggression. Under pressure from the well-covered rebels, Gaddafi's position weakened. When he lost control of most Libyan territory, he sent messages to the Libyan rebels asking to start talks about forming a coalition government.

On hearing of Gaddafi's plea for a unity government, the rebels' information minister Mahmoud Shamam said, "even if Gaddafi personally calls me and asks for negotiations I would never talk to him. The rebels do not negotiate with criminals and killers, and prison, not talks, lie ahead for Gaddafi." The rebels saw their struggle as a Column C campaign to destroy Gaddafi's power once and for all.

The military action taken by NATO and the Arab League had succeeded in forcing Gaddafi to lay down his arms. In his desperation, Gaddafi would have welcomed negotiation with his adversaries, though he was not in a position to bargain for his life. Why didn't the international forces negotiate? They could have gotten whatever they asked for! But it appeared that the ultimate intention of the international forces had always been to get rid of Gaddafi, ending the conflict by eviscerating the enemy. Gaddafi had lost, and, for better or for worse, the rebels and the international community had conspired to vanquish him.[9]

Vanquishing is a fight to the end. It is about besting the opponent until they are powerless to prevail. Vanquishing, whether it is wielded by those in power or by those with less power, is the realm of Column C.

The vanquishing approach to conflict consists of many of the same methods as power building. Both approaches can be carried out with nonviolent direct action, with violent methods, or with threats of violence. To an observer, it may be impossible to know whether a particular power-building campaign is an act of vanquishing or an act of power building. It is only the aim of the approach that characterizes it as either Column B, power building, or Column C, vanquishing. The aim of vanquishing is not to achieve a symmetry of power or to make problem solving possible. Rather, its purpose is to dominate the opposition and to render it powerless.

How can it be that a power-building approach resembles a vanquishing approach to such a degree? Why would activities designed to build power and shift to Column A be equally effective in dominating or destroying? It is because domination too requires building power—not to match the power of the other but to have *more* power than the other. The group that chooses vanquishing aims to use its power to take away the other's power. The group wants to win, once and for all.

In Figure 3.4, the methods of vanquishing are lined up in Column C. Workers, students, or poor people may wield Column C actions against official authorities with an uprising, a rebellion, or an attempted takeover. A punishing response by management or official authorities would also be in Column C. When this happens in a society, we call it the struggle between repression and revolution. Among countries, we call it a war.

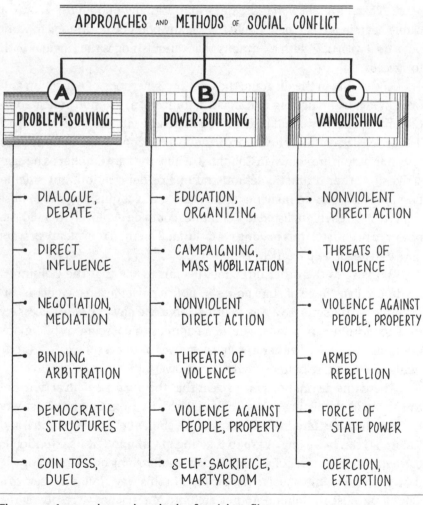

Figure 3.4: Approaches and methods of social conflict

Column C is the source of the Boston Tea Party and Donald Trump's immigration program. It is also the rationale for the prison abolition movement. It is where anti-fascist and anti-capitalist movements act and where the more committed pro-gun and anti-gun groups build their strategies. (You can assess for yourself whether any of these groups would be more successful or more righteous using the methods of Column B to build the power to get to Column A. But their current approaches do by definition place them in Column C.)

Whether consciously or not, groups that take action in Column C are working on the assumption that a deal with the adversary will never take place. They have answered the question, "Can my opponent become a viable negotiation partner? Could they at any point be positioned to work out a deal with us?" with a certainty that vanquishing is the singular path to success.

Notice that in the diagram, the Column B methods of education and organizing, campaigning and mass mobilization, are not indicated in Column C, but they could be deployed there as well. The tools of nonviolent action can certainly be used to vanquish the opposition. Self-sacrifice and martyrdom are shown in Column B, where they are familiar as hunger strikes or other dramatic demonstrations of deprivation, but suicide bombings are easy to imagine in the service of vanquishing the opposition. Armed rebellion, listed in Column C, could be deployed to build the power to negotiate, thus making it a Column B method too; plenty of wars end with negotiated treaties.

Working in the other direction, it's fair to say that the Column C method called "force of state power"—police power against civilians, for example—would not be a way to bring about the power parity necessary for successful negotiations. The same applies to coercion. While many methods can be used either to equalize power or to overpower, these particular methods are better suited to overpowering.

These fine distinctions make clear that the *purpose* of an action, not the action itself, distinguishes Column B activity from Column C activity. But decoding the thinking behind a group's choice between Column B and Column C can be vexing. A group is acting in Column C if its intention is to neutralize the power of the opposition, establishing or maintaining the power to unilaterally resolve the conflict. In this way, Column C serves a similar purpose to Column A: they are both approaches to resolving the issues underlying the conflict. In Column C, the needs or desires of one party are addressed, and in Column A, joint problem solving addresses the needs or desires of all parties. Column B action, on the other hand, does not resolve a conflict. It equalizes the power relations among parties to the conflict, laying the groundwork for resolution through the joint problem-solving methods of Column A.

Every approach to social conflict can be located in one of these three categories: sitting down to resolve a conflict together, fighting for space at the negotiating table, or vanquishing an opponent. How do groups choose among them? It is about *power*—weaker groups mobilizing power to match the structural, economic, or military power of the decision makers. It is about *structural barriers*—formidable obstacles that can get in the way of a group's chosen strategy. It is about *principle*—groups filtering their strategic choices through their values. And it is about *biases*—the inclinations and influences that unwittingly cause groups to circumvent effective, available, principled strategy in favor of familiar, comfortable, reassuring, unexamined strategy.

We now enter Section II, a deep-dive into these four factors influencing a group's choice of approach to conflict.

FACTORS IN CHOOSING TO TALK OR FIGHT

If you are ready to dive into a discussion of power, by all means jump ahead to page 58. But if you'd first like a nitty-gritty review of the model as presented so far, please read on.

Columns A and B

What's the difference between Column A and Column B? In Column A, opponents use joint consensual methods to resolve their conflict. They negotiate. In Column B, a group acts unilaterally against its opponents to build power.

You can distinguish Column A activity from a Column B activity by both the purpose and the nature of the activity. Column A and Column B have distinct qualities, so it's easy to remember the difference. The quintessential Column A activity is negotiation, and the centerpiece of Column B activity is protest.

Sure, some Column A actions resemble protest, and some Column B actions resemble reconciliation. For example, running for office is in Column A, since competing in an election means freely participating in an agreed upon activity with others who are also participating freely. *With* here doesn't mean that competing candidates have friendly relations. It means they are participating in a joint consensual process for the purpose of resolving the question of which candidate should serve in office.

An example of a Column B action that you might think of as more "joint and consensual" is circulating petitions for a legislative or corporate campaign. Gathering signatures to get on a ballot is one thing, since all sides participate according to agreed-upon rules, but gathering signatures to petition an elected official or corporate executive to change a policy is not joint consensual activity. It is an action taken by groups against other individuals or groups for the purpose of building power.

When a group has built its power in Column B, and its power is roughly balanced with that of its opponent, the two groups can "meet" in Column A to work out a resolution to the problem. Because they are now engaged in a negotiation of equals, the groups have a chance to resolve the conflict by satisfying the needs and desires that underlie it.

Columns B and C

What's the difference between Column B and Column C? They are so much alike! In Column B, groups use unilateral nonconsensual methods against their opponents to build power. They are building their power to make it possible to go to Column A—that is, to resolve the conflict together with their opponents. In Column C, groups use the same methods as Column B—community organizing, protest, nonviolent direct action, or even taking up arms—but they are on a different journey. Their action is intended to neutralize their opponents, to metaphorically, if not physically, trample them. Column C activity is power-building activity of the sort that leaves one group with all the marbles. Column C action means joint consensual action to prevail over an opponent, clearing the way to resolve the conflict unilaterally.

Does that mean that groups in Column C are trying to kill people? Possibly, but violence and killing can occur in Column B too. Plenty of battles, large and small, end with a truce and a treaty. Column B and Column C activities have different purposes though. Groups in Column C are trying to reduce the power of their opponents to insignificance. If a group or social movement sets out to abolish the fossil fuel industry without its consent, that group is acting in Column C—even if every owner, investor, scientist, and worker in the fossil fuel industry lands a good job in the renewable energy sector. If, on the other hand, the same group sets out to pressure the fossil fuel industry into making incremental changes through legislative or corporate policy change, that group would be acting in Column B.

The actions groups take in Columns B and C may seem similar, but they are going different places. Groups in Column B are building power to take over to Column A for joint resolution. Groups in Column C are building power to prevail over their opponents and resolve their conflict unilaterally. In short, power is built in Column B and Column C, and conflicts are resolved in Column A and Column C.

For groups that define their active wants as the entire menu of justice for all, winning requires either a Column C strategy or a chain of Column B campaigns in a long-term struggle to change the fundamental arrangements of social power. Resistance must be constant. Civil rights organizer Ella Baker said, "Until the killing of black men, black mothers' sons, becomes as important to the rest of the country as the killing of a white mother's son—we who believe in freedom cannot rest until this happens."[1] This incremental use of mobilized power by the weak to change the prevailing arrangement of institutionalized power constitutes one of the most powerful applications of Column B.

Do groups in Column B and Column C know which column they are in? Not necessarily. In our organizations and communities, as in society, changemakers frequently take action without a theory of changemaking or without a clear strategic plan. The model described in this book can enable you to decode the strategies of groups in conflict, whether or not those strategies are intentional. In addition, the model can guide you to develop your own conflict strategy with awareness and intention, maximizing the chances the conflict will be resolved in a way that gets you what you need and desire.

Which Strategy Is the Best Strategy?

In Section II, we dig into four key factors that influence a group's choice of Column A, B, or C approaches. Sometimes a conflict is located entirely in Column A, and at other times a group will engage a sequence of approaches. A group may simultaneously negotiate while building power, like a group of education advocates who recruit new members to build their ranks at the same time as they negotiate with the school board for improvements in the curriculum.

On what basis do groups make these decisions about whether to talk in Column A or fight in Column B or Column C? They do this, consciously or unconsciously, by considering power dynamics, structural barriers, values and principles, and biases and inclinations toward one approach or another.

Consciously or unconsciously, opponents consider *who is more and less powerful* as they choose their approach to a conflict. Consciously or unconsciously, their choices are limited by *structural barriers* like money, sexism, and other entrenched social, political, and cultural realities. Structural barriers may prevent a weaker group from enacting the strategy that, in light of a power analysis, would best achieve their goals. Groups

ANALYSIS TOOLS
FOR CHOOSING COLUMN A, B, OR C

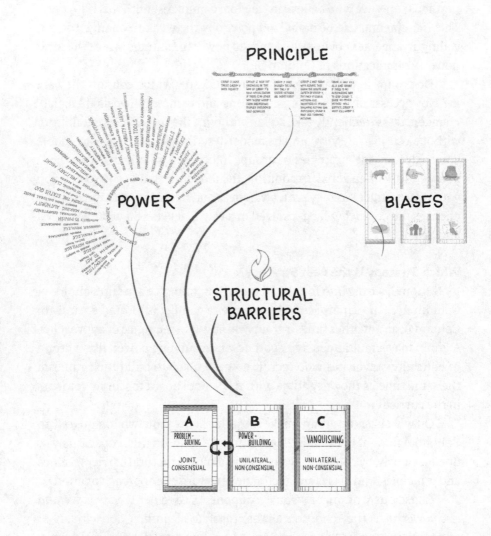

Figure II.1: Analysis tools for choosing Column A, B, or C

choose or refuse to engage in certain approaches to conflict not only for their strategic utility but for their harmony with their *values*, whether or not they have considered those values consciously. Finally, strategic decisions are influenced by unintentional, unconscious *predispositions, inclinations, habits,* and *biases*. We each have them; all groups have them. The last chapter in Section II, chapter 8, is all about these biases.

Because the influence of our biases always functions below the level of our awareness, our strategic thinking has most to gain by exploring this factor. When we get to chapter 8, you will meet a cast of change-seeking characters who make better or worse choices about which approach to take. Each brings a set of biases to their analysis, and learning about them may raise your awareness of your own biases in approaching conflict.

Now we can dive into Power.

CHAPTER 4

Power

You won't be surprised to hear that I'm a longtime member of my local food co-op. For decades, we lived just up the block, and I would drop in once or even twice a day. The co-op was practically my pantry. I knew all the stock people and the check-out clerks by name. It's a small store, so some larger items are displayed out on the sidewalk—jugs of water, pumpkins, and, in winter, ice melt. There were times when I'd run down, grab a jug of water, and pay for it later.

For years I was unaware of the sense of entitlement that involved. I could grab those water jugs without fear only because my face reads "trust me." Before I understood that consciously, I knew it intuitively. This is not because of my beauty; I look like a mashup of Gertrude Stein and Rand Paul with the fashion sense of Bernie Sanders. But I move through the world expecting to be trusted and, apparently, in my progressive, middle-class, queer-familiar, mixed-race neighborhood, I am. I am a person categorized as white, I benefit from white privilege, and my gestures have the certainty of middle-class entitlement. Surely everyone knows I wouldn't steal a jug of water!

Then one day, I lingered on that sidewalk, as I'd done a million times, and idly lifted a jug of water while chatting with an African American neighbor. Suddenly, it burst into my awareness: my Black neighbor would not have stolen the water jug either, but she could not count on the pas- sersby, or even the friendly store clerks, to recognize her inherent honesty as they did mine. I had a superpower that she did not have. My white-skin privilege protected me from suspicious neighbors and vigilant checkout clerks.

What Is Power?

Philosophers, feminists, and sociologists variously understand social power to be about control, domination, oppression, violence, choice, influence, capacity, and agency. Definitions include the ability to create, the ability to change things, and the ability to produce an intended effect. It is the ability to get what you and your loved ones want or need. It is the ability to get a group of people to join you to produce the effect that you intend. It is the ability to get an opponent to do what they would not otherwise do.[1]

For the purpose of this book, in which we're examining power in social conflict, we can define power as *the ability of a group to meet a specific objective despite barriers posed by another group or groups.* I am powerful enough to steal a jug of water from the co-op without fear of clerks or cops. My neighbor is not.

Like my own lack of awareness about the privilege that let me steal with impunity, a group's sense of power may be intuitive rather than conscious. But those employees, neighbors, and citizens who strategize *intentionally* about change will base their strategy on a conscious assessment of power relations. If their power is balanced with the power of their opponents, they will talk with their opponents, negotiate, and try to work out a deal. These are the joint consensual problem-solving methods we call Column A.

If the opponents are more powerful, the weaker group will choose the unilateral power-building methods of Column B. They will mobilize sufficient power to get their opponents' attention and then keep building their power through protest, battle, increased numbers, and louder voices until their power balances that of their opponents. When power is balanced, they return to Column A to negotiate a resolution. The negotiated resolution may be temporary, or it may settle the issue for good.

If the weaker group faces an opponent so evil or irrational that future negotiation is unrealistic or, in the weaker group's estimation, morally unfathomable, the weaker group will still choose unilateral power-building methods. But in this circumstance, they will not be fighting for the purpose of returning to Column A. Their struggle and tactics may resemble Column B, but under these circumstances, we call their approach Column C, because its function is different; a Column B strategy seeks to mobilize equal power, while, in Column C, a group works to vanquish the power of the opposition once and for all.

I know an activist named Jethro Heiko whose happy place is Column B. I met him at the start of the second Iraq war, when he was organizing soldiers and veterans to protest US foreign policy. Jethro would say that his job was to be in Column B or Column C, mobilizing against a powerful opponent, and that if and when deal-making time arrived, someone else who likes negotiating deals could step into Column A. He'd learned this about himself, he said, during the fight to save the oldest major league baseball stadium in America.

Boston's Fenway Park was built in 1912. In 1999, the Red Sox's owners announced it was time to build a new stadium. Most of Fenway Park would be demolished, with one bit of land remaining to house a baseball museum. The rest of the ballpark would be turned into condos.

Nostalgic Red Sox fans were enraged, and community groups began to organize, lobbying the city council and thinking up ways to save the stadium. Neighborhood groups concerned about the new development made themselves visible at the ballgames, where they handed out flyers and gathered signatures on petitions to preserve the old stadium. They gave the Red Sox a run for their money, and for years the franchise owners struggled.

During these years, Jethro was the director of community organizing at Fenway Community Development Corporation. Fenway CDC had organized hard in the neighborhood around the stadium to harness the anger of citizens concerned about the impact of development, the expense to taxpayers, and the loss of their beloved old ballpark. The protests organized by Fenway CDC and other community groups finally got the attention of the Red Sox owners, who invited representatives of the city and the community to talk about a deal.

The owners spoke. Representatives of the city spoke. Jethro's boss spoke. But the owners were not ready to stand down. They still wanted to destroy Fenway Park and build a new stadium. On their way back to the Fenway CDC office, Jethro's boss said, "I'm handing the baton back to you, Jethro. Gather your people and get back to the streets. Those owners don't get it. We need more people, more numbers. Let's build our side up so that next time they'll have to listen to us; they'll have to say yes to keeping Fenway."

Jethro had led the group's plays in Column B. When it first seemed that their power had risen, the community groups had joined the owners in Column A, where Jethro's boss dug into the negotiating role. But when he realized that the owners still had a considerably better hand, he asked

Jethro to go back to Column B to work with community members to build more power.

This back-and-forth worked. In 2002, the owners caved, selling the Red Sox to new owners committed to preserving the old stadium. They repaired and refurbished it, added seats, and, as you probably know, the 2013 and 2018 Red Sox won their eighth and ninth world series at Fenway Park.

The Balance of Social Power

In the opening chapter, we defined conflict as a situation when your people need something but the other side isn't giving it up. Your side needs to figure out how to get it. You need to determine whether and how to approach the other side. Be it intentionally or unconsciously, groups often make this determination by assessing the power dynamics of the conflict.

Groups like Fenway CDC intentionally make strategic choices based on a power analysis. Their understanding of power is clear enough, and they can measure it well enough to ascertain whether they have enough power to negotiate. They are able to spot symmetrical and asymmetrical power relations. They have a definition of power that enables them to figure out who is stronger and who is the underdog.

Other groups make strategic choices without a conscious analysis of who has how much power. They rely on habits, inclinations, biases, fears, social pressure of one kind or another, and other forces that influence strategy in the absence of consciousness and intention. This isn't ideal. Smart strategy benefits from an awareness of our own biases, an issue we will examine more deeply in chapter 8.

How does a group go about this intentional determination of who has more or less power? When Cody, the organizer trying to win sick leave for workers, was finally called in by management to negotiate, how did he know whether the workers had as much power as management? How do citizens working to keep an incinerator out of their neighborhood know when they have as much power as the landowner who intends to build it? How did the Black Panthers know that they were failing to build the power necessary to upend inequality?

If you were a kid in 1995 or since, you may be intimate with the 800+ species of Japanese anime characters who inhabit Pokémon World. Even if you aren't, you probably know of them, since, by 2020, Pokémon video games, TV shows, movies, and merchandise made up the highest-grossing media franchise in the world.

Pokémon characters are always seeking opportunities to conquer regions beyond their own. They constantly size each other up, estimating the other's power. They do this both for their own safety and for purposes of potential conquest.

How do the Pokémon estimate each other's power? Well, each individual Pokémon is coded as having or missing certain attributes. Each has a gender assignment of female, male, or no gender. Each has a size and a level of shininess, and the spots on the little cases that serve as homes to the Pokémon differ in number and positioning. Pokémon have quantifiable abilities, and the "nature" of an individual Pokémon is defined by just a single one of these abilities: hardy, lonely, brave, adamant, naughty, bold, docile, relaxed, impish, lax, timid, hasty, serious, jolly, naive, modest, mild, quiet, bashful, rash, calm, gentle, sassy, careful, or quirky. This quantifiable ability is one of a Pokémon's "constant" attributes.

One Pokémon can get help predicting how another will behave by factoring together the calendar date, the beverage drunk most recently by that other, and the other's constant attributes. An intrepid Pokémon can get access to the Pokémon hidden power calculator and determine precisely how much and what type of power a hostile Pokémon has.

I mention these objective and measurable currencies of Pokémon power because estimating the power of a human group is not so simple. It would be useful to reduce all forms of social-change power to a single currency, like Pokémon power attributes for people, but in human conflicts, it's never so easy to judge power. Fortunately, we don't need a single currency to measure power or any absolute measure of power. We only need to determine whether a given group has sufficient power to negotiate.

We saw in chapter 3 that groups move from Column A to Column B as necessary to build power, and from Column B back to Column A when they have equalized power enough to facilitate an acceptable negotiation outcome. Like the Fenway activists, groups make this determination by asking, "Do we have enough power to get our interests met through negotiation?" Power is a group's ability to get what it wants when somebody is in the way. It is the currency that gives us a fair shot at getting our interests met through negotiation. When our power is equal to our opponent's power, we have the possibility of getting what we want. We can sharpen our question by asking, "Do we have at least as much power as they do?" (See Figure 4.1.) But how do we know? We need a way to figure out the answer. Let's start with an easily measured currency of power—the mighty dollar.

Say you've run out of gas with $30 to spend. You want to fill up to avoid the need for a stop later. Your tank holds ten gallons of gas, and the gas station charges $3 per gallon. You insert your plastic money, you pump your gas, and you drive off. Why isn't there a conflict? Because you, the gas station attendant, and the company that employs them all got what you wanted without any objection from each other.

Conflict, on the other hand, occurs when someone else is holding the keys to your happiness. Say you only have $20 and you want to fill up your ten-gallon tank. Would you ask the attendant to please give you $30 of gas for just $20? If you did, there would be a conflict! You want to fill your tank, and the attendant and the gas company don't want people to take stuff without paying the listed price. Sure, they could fill up your tank for free if they chose to. But there are rules that say there's no stealing, plus if they make an exception for one person, everyone will want free gas. The attendant wants you to pay your money, pump your gas, and leave so that they don't have to call the cops. They could call the cops, of course; there's a secret button under the counter. But they don't want the hassle.

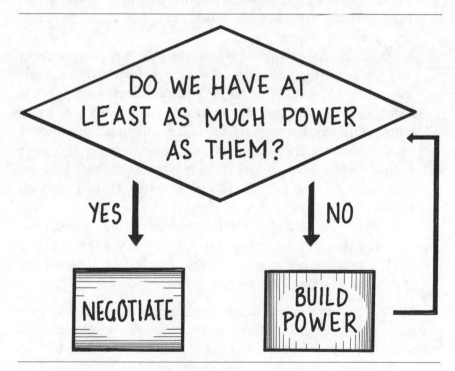

Figure 4.1: The deluxe power-building cycle

You want something, and someone else is preventing you from getting it. As usual in a conflict, the other guy also wants something—for you to pay or go away, and you are preventing them from fulfilling that desire.

Who has more power now, you or the gas station attendant? Or are your power and the attendant's power balanced?

Power is balanced when the groups can both get what they're contending for. We can formulate a set of questions that any group can use to make this determination. To do so, let's take another example, this time of two nature-loving neighborhood clubs. The Sparks celebrate May Day by dancing around a favorite cherry tree. The Rockets hold the key to the gate for the field where the cherry tree grows. The Sparks are developing a strategy to gain access to the tree. They ask these questions to determine whether their power balances the Rockets' power. If the power is balanced, they will try to negotiate with the Rockets.

1. *Do the Rockets have access to what the Sparks want?* In this case, the Sparks want access to the cherry tree. Do the Rockets have the thing that the Sparks want, in the sense that they control the Sparks' access to it? Do they have the key to the gate for the field where the Sparks' cherry tree is flowering?

2. *Are the Rockets able to give the Sparks access?* Do they have the ability and agency to grant the Sparks the thing they want? The Rockets may have the key to the gate for the field, but if there is a bigger tree blocking access to the Sparks' favorite tree, and the only good access is from a neighboring property, the Rockets may not be able to give the Sparks access. The Sparks may have the wrong target.

3. *Are the Rockets willing to give the Sparks access?* Do they have any motivation to give the Sparks access to the tree? Do they have any reason not to?

4. *Are the Rockets willing and able to give the Sparks access now?* Assuming they have access to the tree, are theoretically able to give the Sparks access, and are willing to grant it, is there any obstacle that would delay their ability to give the Sparks the access?

If the answer to the first or second question is no, the Sparks have the wrong target. They should leave the Rockets alone! Or recruit them as allies in the struggle for the May Day tree!

If the Sparks can answer all four questions in the affirmative, they have sufficient power to negotiate. They have a credible course ahead in working jointly with the Rockets. Resolution of the May Day tree conflict does not require the reordering of power.

You might be thinking, "Wait a minute. If the Rockets are willing and able to give the Sparks access to their tree, then there's no conflict." But then you probably remembered that frequently conflict comes from a lack of confidence and awareness that working out solutions together is possible.

This is one source of conflict among groups with balanced power. The problem may be a lack of the skill, knowledge, or confidence necessary to negotiate. Or the problem may be a misperception of the balance of power. Every conflict is, by definition, based on one or both of these two predicaments:

> Group Y has the power to remove the obstacles to the object of group X's need or desire without forfeiting any of its own essential interests, but this is not evident to group Y, and it may not be evident to group X either; or group Y has more power than group X.

Now you may be thinking, "Wait a minute. The fact that group Y has more power than group X doesn't mean that group Y won't be willing to negotiate. There are good people who have power, and they may be ready to give us what we need without being forced to." In chapter 3, we read statements by Frederick Douglass and Dr. King explaining how unusual that is but noting that it does occasionally happen. When we meet people willing to meet the needs of others voluntarily we will refer to them as Robin Hoods. We'll have more to say about Robin Hoods later.

Another Powerful Measure of Power

The factors that determine the balance of power are subtle and dynamic. The very dynamics of a negotiation shift the flows of power, so there needs to be some give on the definition of "balance." If power is roughly balanced at the moment we choose an approach to a conflict, we still need to be vigilant about maintaining power parity, to make sure we are not wasting our time in Column A. What a tenuous project this measuring of the balance of power can be!

In 1981, Roger Fisher and William Ury published the first edition of their still bestselling book *Getting to Yes,* introducing an elegant theory of conflict resolution called "interest-based negotiation." In this approach, preparation for a negotiation includes an assessment of the parties' relative power. Millions of lawyers, mediators, business dealmakers, legislators, policy advocates, and general readers have since used one of Fisher and Ury's most popular tools to make this assessment. Getting to know this tool, called "BATNA" (best alternative to a negotiated agreement), will strengthen our ability to determine the balance of power in a conflict.[2]

In interest-based negotiation, group X listens with curiosity to group Y, discerning and learning Y's needs, wishes, and concerns. Group X, in turn, tells group Y what their own priorities and concerns are. Together, groups X and Y brainstorm possible solutions that address the needs of both groups. In the worst case, the negotiation ends with a deal that's bearable to both sides, and, in the best case, they forge an agreement that gives both groups everything they wanted and more.

But sometimes one or all the parties to a conflict can't get a bearable deal. Their needs cannot be met through negotiation. When that happens, what do they do? If they're negotiating with a leasing company to rent office space, they look at other buildings. If they're union workers at a factory, they may call a strike. If they belong to a community group participating in mediation with rival community groups, they give up on the mediation and take action independently.

In the 2010s, the city of Seattle struggled to house all of its residents. Activists, unhoused people, and elected officials called on local industry to help fund affordable housing. Amazon, one of Seattle's biggest employers, was not willing to pay its share. The city administration needed to determine whether to ask Amazon to negotiate or to act unilaterally against Amazon in an attempt to get them to back the housing fund. To choose the most effective course of action, they needed to determine who had more power.

You could measure Amazon's power in terms of money, real estate, market share, brand recognition, social networks, and the privilege of the second richest person on earth, Jeff Bezos, the straight white man who owns the company. City power was measurable in terms of the mandate of the votes that got its members elected, the time remaining until the next election, how formidable their forthcoming election contests appeared, the relative strength or weakness of the tax base, the size of Seattle's budget, the city's real estate assets, and its tourism and other industries. Seattle's resources also included the ability of city council members and the mayor to work together for a common cause, and their individual and combined privilege, money, and negotiation skill.

When you compare the power of the parties to a conflict, you're frequently comparing apples to oranges. But watch how BATNA can help.

If we are Seattle and we can't get a bearable deal from Amazon, we face a set of options. We could give in, at least for now, and continue to lead a city where people sleep in shelters, on the couches of friends and relations, or on the street. We could play another local powerhouse, Microsoft, off against Amazon. We could instead work with community groups to pressure Amazon directly by organizing a boycott of their popular consumer products. We could work with employee groups to pressure Amazon from within. We could end city contracts with Amazon. If we can't get a bearable deal from Amazon, we will have a long list of options from which to choose.

In interest-based negotiation, you don't wait until a negotiation fails to think through your alternatives. You do that thinking in advance. Before even trying to work out a deal, you think through all of your alternatives, all of the actions you could take if you fail to reach a deal with the other party or parties. You then enter the negotiation having already determined the most favorable course of action you could take without needing consent from your opponents.

Let's take a step back to the example of the group negotiating with a leasing company for new office space. Imagine we are that group. What are our unilateral alternatives? Could we consider getting a lease in another building? Could we stay where we are for another couple of years, if we had to? Could we make good on that indoor gym idea we've batted around, making it more appealing to stay in our current space?

In the example of the factory union, do we suppose the workers would support a strike? What if they don't? What about a work stoppage or a sick-out, where scores of workers stay home on a designated day?

Just as a movement campaigner would map out a strategy before taking action, an interest-based negotiator would anticipate the range of possible scenarios before negotiating. They would pick their best possible course of action should deal-making fail. They would hold this in their mind as their best alternative to a negotiated agreement—their BATNA.

But here's the kicker: interest-based negotiation tells us that if you are in Seattle city hall mapping out a negotiation plan you probably aren't seriously considering boycotting Amazon or negotiating with Microsoft. Rather, your *awareness* of your BATNA, your best alternative, makes it more likely that you won't ever have to use it.

This awareness mechanism works in several ways. Before you agree to any deal, you can compare the would-be deal to your BATNA; your comfort with the BATNA you identify in advance sets a standard below which you will not go. You will be better positioned to avoid being pushed or bullied into a bad deal. Your awareness that you can walk away from the negotiation and enact your BATNA gives you a stronger negotiating position; this means you will work harder to get a better deal.

Since you will not agree to a resolution worse than your BATNA, having a good BATNA works in your favor. The better your BATNA, the stronger you'll feel negotiating, and the better the value of any deal will be, at least for you, because you'll make sure of that. You'll negotiate knowing that you could organize a strike at any moment; in fact, if the union membership votes now to commit to a strike if and when negotiations fail, you've made your BATNA even stronger. This puts you in position to get an even stronger agreement.

Figuring out your BATNA is a wonderfully clever process. In trying to determine your best alternative to negotiated agreement, you piece together the strongest possible, most creative combination of the currencies of power you've got.

Your opponents have their BATNA too, whether or not they've thought about it. The stronger their BATNA, the better deal they will get—just like you.

In other words, the group with the better backup plan is more powerful. Elegant, no?

Your BATNA as a Real-Life Option

Interest-based negotiation teaches us to be aware of our alternatives and our opponents' alternatives. We are advised to improve our BATNA and maybe even take action to weaken the BATNA of the other side. But what if it comes time to follow through with our BATNA? What if management digs in or Amazon won't budge?

BATNA provides an exit ramp from interest-based negotiation and leads to a world of powerful alternative possibilities that are sometimes precisely the best way to solve a problem. To negotiators, that exit ramp is theoretical. It is where bombs are dropped, and a negotiator's work is to prevent the dropping of bombs.

But BATNA is a legitimate choice, not merely a tool for improving the outcome of negotiation. Talking is not the only option. To factory workers, rival civic groups, and concerned Seattle residents and elected officials, the alternatives are very real.

Here's another Philadelphia story: for twenty-seven years, beginning in the late twentieth century and continuing into the twenty-first, local activists pressured the mayor and city council to create a public access television station. Philadelphia, the home of cable TV giant Comcast, was the last big-city holdout without public access cable. Multiple generations of activists spoke with the mayor and lobbied council members, but these elected officials had a great BATNA—do nothing. This attractive alternative eliminated the city's motivation to strike a deal with the activists. Sure, they realized that the public interest cable supporters could mobilize a small number of concerned citizens, but that prospect didn't frighten the Philadelphia city officials.

For years, the activists' BATNA of "organize grassroots support" was no match for the city's rock-hard BATNA of "do nothing." It cost those city officials much less to do nothing than it would have cost the activists to organize support at a scale big enough to win. It wasn't enough for the activists to know their best alternative to lobbying the city. The currencies of power available to the less powerful—in this example, a masterful grip on the techniques of organizing and mobilizing people—is worth little at the negotiating table during the early stages of a conflict. Its worth grows away from the negotiations, in strategy meetings and in the streets. The power of alternatives *away* from the negotiating table is a mighty currency indeed.

The cable activists started in Column A with the city and got no deal. They shifted to Column B, and then moved back and forth between A and B, sometimes even negotiating and protesting simultaneously. Politicians began to get the sense they could lose votes, and business leaders started to worry that they could lose customers. When the power of the activists began to frighten the elected officials and business leaders, those city and Comcast leaders realized that the value of their alternatives to negotiating with the activists had plummeted. They hadn't lost, but they would now be facing equals. It was time to talk.

After years of op-eds, street demonstrations, and direct-action protests, the protesters were finally invited in for serious negotiations with the mayor and Comcast, and the activists said, "Yes, thank you!" Philly now has a thriving public access television network with a stunning studio, funded in large part by Comcast and governed by rules negotiated between the activists, the city, and Comcast.[3]

Although the concept of BATNA was invented as a tool for improving negotiations, actually carrying out one's BATNA adds a world of possibilities to a negotiator's repertoire for dealing with conflict. It actually adds two worlds: all of the unilateral power-building methods of Column B and the same methods and more in Column C, where the aim becomes vanquishing the opponent.

The Column ABC framework liberates BATNA from its strategic but limited role at the negotiating table and gives equal appreciation to its impressive value away from the table. Negotiators and proponents of dialogue need to own their BATNA strategies, because sometimes when we can't get a good enough deal at the table, when our leverage or the power our cause has accrued is insufficient, we need to find a fitting strategy for building greater power. We need that power precisely in order to get a deal, to restore stability and good relationships where possible, and, if necessary, to consolidate gains for the next stage in our conflict or struggle.

BATNA remains an ideal gauge of the relative power among parties to a conflict. Column B and C are names for BATNA in action.

We have theorized the dynamics of power, but we have not described its nature. We are still talking about social power as if it's a collection of pebbles or rubles piled on a tabletop. In the next chapter we will examine power directly, currency by currency.

CHAPTER 5

Currencies of Power

Philosophers have created a range of taxonomies for social power. They have played with the distinction between having power and exercising it. They have examined tangible forms of power, such as financial wealth and armies, and intangible kinds of power like negotiation skill and social networks. Some feminist writers define power in terms of domination and oppression, or *power over*, whereas others understand power as potential that is either inherent or emergent in a party. Power is many things to many people, and it has spawned a library's worth of theories.[1] For the purposes of this book, we have defined power as the ability of a group to meet a specific objective despite barriers posed by another group or groups.

What does power look like, practically speaking? We can think of power as an arrangement of forces that enable a group to get what it wants. Philosopher Michel Foucault is our guide here, describing power as "not an institution, and not a structure; neither is it a certain strength we are endowed with; it is the name that one attributes to a complex strategical situation in a particular society." Power is a "multiplicity of force relations," a process "which, through ceaseless struggles and confrontations, transforms, strengthens, or even reverses [those force relations]; as the support which these force relations find in one another, thus forming a chain or a system."[2]

Let's look at this notion of power as a multiplicity of forces transforming themselves in a sort of chain reaction.

In 2019, opponents of Trump's immigration program called on big banks to stop financing detention centers that profited from the separation of the members of migrant families. When organizers celebrated a big win, Representative Alexandria Ocasio-Cortez (AOC), who was one of their boosters, tweeted, "Huge update: JP Morgan & Wells Fargo have announced that they will no longer fund private prisons. How did this happen? Through organizing people & public pressure! Everyday folks began paying attention to who was funding for-profit prisons and family separation + acted on it."[3]

Although AOC was right to give credit where she did, the full picture is more complicated. Yes, the achievement stemmed in part from the work of everyday people angered by the news and it was, in large part, the result of organized campaigns engaging thousands of citizens and customers. But another major factor was AOC herself wielding a powerful megaphone from inside Congress. Her election itself had been the result of a door-to-door canvassing operation, AOC's powerful social media presence, and her performance in public debates and at campaign rallies. The grassroots power that coalesced around AOC's election emerged from the mass engagement that followed the election of Donald Trump. That engagement tapped the organizing experience of veterans of recent mobilizations, including Occupy Wall Street, the Movement for Black Lives, and the Women's March. Trump's election unleashed new outrage, and the momentum of grassroots campaigns strengthened these interlocking currencies of power.

In other words, a multiplicity of forces transformed themselves in a sort of chain reaction. This arrangement of forces enabled a group of citizens and leaders to get what they wanted. We can call each of these forces a currency of power.

We can fit all of these currencies of social power into three categories: *structural power*, *resources on hand*, and *potential power*.

Trump used *structural power* when he leveraged his office to separate families. The banks used their wealth—the power of *resources on hand*—to invest in and profit from the detention centers.

On the other side of the picture, AOC also had access to structural power and used it; her tweets went viral in part because of the prominence of her official position as a member of Congress. Her social media presence itself had become an additional source of power in the form of resources on hand.

The activists who ran the campaigns that got JP Morgan and Wells Fargo to pull their financing from the detention centers used their resources on hand to power their organizing. These resources included lists of potential recruits, strategy know-how, technology infrastructure, and the backing of private donors. We can think of resources on hand as tradeable currencies. But these currencies were useful only when *potential power* was mobilized—that is, when people, strategy, technology, and money were organized into a winning campaign.

Structural power, such as the positional power of elected office or the way money is distributed in this country, is like gravity; unless the conflict is about a group's desire to neutralize structural power itself as a currency of power, it will remain intact throughout the course of the conflict.

Resources on hand, such as networks, knowledge, and cash, circulate more freely. Some groups have more, some have less, and when it comes to intangible resources, it is generally possible for any group to increase the resource power that it has.

At rest, *potential power* does not effect change, but pressure from structural power can activate the transformation of potential power into both mobilized power (e.g., by motivating more people to join a struggle) and increased resources (e.g., by encouraging people to become financial supporters).

To illustrate these three categories we can imagine two little kids playing on a seesaw (or, if you prefer, a teeter-totter). They are pictured in Figure 5.1. The kids are good buddies, and they know how to cooperate, even though Jamie is older than Foluke. Jamie goes up and Foluke comes down. Foluke pushes off and Jamie comes back down. They get tired and tap their toes on the ground to stay balanced. They seem to be equals.

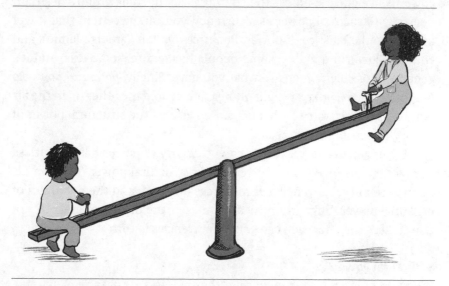

Figure 5.1: Seesaw

After a bit of seesawing and a bit of tip-tapping to stay in balance, Jamie, who is not only older but bigger than Foluke, lets her weight keep her end of the seesaw on the ground. At first this is fun for Foluke, hanging high in the sky, while Jamie sits at her end and lets Foluke dangle. When at last Foluke complains that it is no longer fun, Jamie pushes off hard with her feet. This gives the seesaw enough bounce for Foluke to reach the ground, knees bent, and Foluke adds her own kinetic energy to the activity.

Who has more power in the seesaw game? At first Jamie has more power, because of her size. Jamie's size is of greatest value when she is sitting still and keeping Foluke in place. But when Jamie kicks off, and physics sends her soaring, Foluke's weight has power too. Foluke's weight combines with Jamie's pushing off to lift Jamie up into the air. When Foluke touches the ground again, Jamie is at her highest point—and now Jamie's potential power is greatest. She is about to cause Foluke to fly back up to the sky.

As long as either child is in the air, their weight will be a currency of power. As long as either child has the use of their quads and their glutes, these too will be currencies of power. And as long as the laws of physics prevail, gravity will be the third currency of power at play in Jamie and Foluke's game of seesaw.

These three types of power exist in social conflict too. *Structural power* is like gravity; unless the conflict is about some group's desire to neutralize structural power as a currency, you can be certain that it will factor into the balance of power. *Resources on hand* are like Jamie's and Foluke's quads and glutes; some people have more, some less, and it's generally possible to increase what you have. Finally, *potential power* is like Jamie's and Foluke's weight. At rest, it can hold the other up in the air, but when it is activated by being pressed against the structural power of gravity, its capabilities increase.

Figure 5.2 makes clear that each category of power has a limitless number of currencies. The currencies of structural power function differently than the currencies of resources on hand, and the dynamics of potential power differ from the dynamics of the first two categories of power. Let's consider each category of currencies in turn.

Structural Power

When Dr. King spoke of conquering "the giant triplets of racism, extreme materialism, and militarism,"[4] he was talking about structural power.

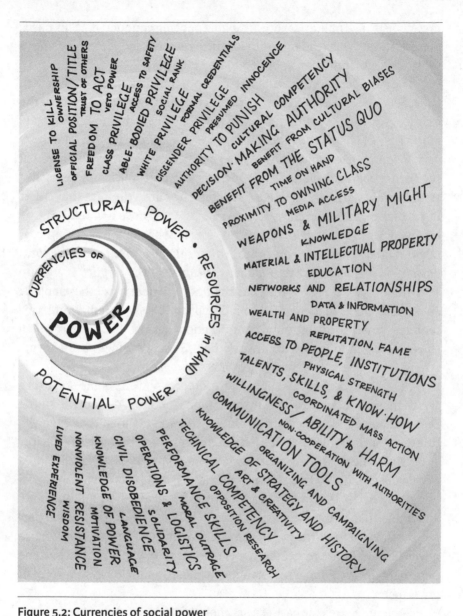

Figure 5.2: Currencies of social power

Structural power is unique in its abiding nature. Under ordinary circumstances, its effects cannot be overcome. But when Dr. King invoked these forces, he offered potent insight into social change. King argued, "When machines and computers, profit motives and property rights, are considered more important than people, the giant triplets of racism, extreme materialism, and militarism are incapable of being conquered." This raises the question: When the opposite is true, when people are valued above profit, can structural power be conquered?

The two Spanish verbs *ser* and *estar* both translate to the English verb *to be*. *Ser* describes a stable condition, such as one's gender identity or the political system of a country, like the English word *is* in the sentence "He is an artistic kid." On the other hand, *estar* is used to refer to a temporary circumstance, like the word *is* in the sentence "She is waiting for you at the corner of Broad and Arch." Gender identity and political systems, like structural power, don't change daily, but they aren't immutable either. Even racism, extreme materialism, militarism, and patriarchy can be changed. By its nature, structural power is stubborn: *unless a conflict is about a group's desire to neutralize structural power itself, the structural power will remain intact throughout the course of the conflict*. If a group that values people above profit has the desire to neutralize these oppressive forces, they will take a Column C approach. As Foucault wrote, this requires "ceaseless struggle and confrontation" against the "support which these force relations find in one another." Such a struggle "transforms, strengthens, or even reverses" their effect.[5]

Most conflict does not challenge structural power. People don't take *ser* changes lightly; these are, by definition, the most disruptive. In the Declaration of Independence, Thomas Jefferson claimed that even the founders of the United States hesitated before starting the revolution: "Prudence, indeed, will dictate that Governments long established should not be changed for light and transient causes; and accordingly all experience hath shewn, that mankind are more disposed to suffer, while evils are sufferable, than to right themselves by abolishing the forms to which they are accustomed." But the gist of the Declaration is, of course, that when a government fails to protect the rights of its people, it may indeed become necessary for the people to defang, neutralize, and abolish that form of government.[6]

Sometimes weaker parties that mobilize to build the power of their group do end up fundamentally changing the arrangements of power in society as a whole. In Tunisia, in 2011, citizen rebels proved so successful in ousting the country's previously entrenched leadership that a government new in both format and personnel replaced the old. This revolutionary change, where the weaker party wrests institutionalized power from the party that monopolizes it, is the "ceaseless struggle" that Foucault writes about, the one that "transforms, strengthens, or even reverses" the prevailing power dynamics. The struggle itself may prove transformational in fundamental ways that alter the power balance among the groups involved.[7]

Structural power is built into our society. It may accrue to an individual from birth and to a group by law or entrenched custom. It is, in many senses, a product of social and economic history. It reflects the systems of authority threaded through our workplaces, communities, and society. The group with the most structural power is able to define the terms of the interaction—to set the rules.

Sometimes it is easy to be grateful for structural power. In June 2016, on the heels of the bomb attack on Pulse, a popular Latinx gay nightclub in Orlando, Florida, Representatives John Lewis, Katherine Clark, and Robin Kelly led a sit-in in Congress. They threatened to remain on the floor of the House until Speaker Paul Ryan allowed a vote on gun control. While this demonstration didn't lead directly to the passing of a law, it lent credibility to citizens' anti–gun violence campaigns. Anyone who opposed American gun violence could be glad that our elected officials had access to the floor of the House. That access is part of the structural power built into the congressional system.

In other cases, of course, we are incensed by the abuse of structural power. The power of concentrated wealth is a familiar source of distress for most of us. So is the power to make the rules or to make decisions, whether this authority is explicit or informal. The state's authority to punish, while less visible to many, is one of the most important currencies of structural power for us to understand.

The authority to punish is an official form of structural power. In the US, only the state—that is, government at all its levels—has the legal power to detain, penalize, or punish an adult. It is this monopoly that gives government its power. The government's power includes the license of its police and military forces to kill, wound, frighten, and threaten, the ability of its courts to mandate detention, penalties, and punishment, and the moral authority of the state. This moral power depends on the degree to which citizens believe that state authority is legitimate and have faith that the state is exercising its authority in accordance with the law. The widespread absence of that legitimacy and of popular faith in government enhances the tension between the state and those most vulnerable to the violence it inflicts, whether intentionally or unintentionally.

Another currency of structural power—one that guides most social transactions—is the social-ranking system. Most of the power that comes from social-ranking systems isn't formal or official. We may not even acknowledge it in our conversations, public or private. Who decides what color to paint the walls? Who is seated at the head table? Who's standing in the center of the front row in the group photo? Sometimes the silence that surrounds this power makes it even greater.

Consider gender: masculine men who were raised as men and continue to move through the world as men are at the top of the hierarchy. Consider race: people who are perceived as white rank highest in our society. Consider socioeconomic class: groups with more education, money, and exposure to culture and art tend to have more power. Informal structural power comes from the value of men in a sexist context, white people in a racist context, wealthy or financially stable people in our class-based culture, and conventionally beautiful people in a society fixated on physical appearance. Think of a low-level corporate employee who is Black, working-class, gender-nonconforming, and eager for a promotion. These intersecting elements of their identity will reduce their power to negotiate with their boss, whereas a middle-class white man brings personal characteristics that may secure his advancement with minimal effort.

When it comes to the currency of whiteness in American, there are written rules and unwritten rules. For example, there are legal regulations guiding the circumstances under which a person is allowed to get government benefits. Eligibility requirements vary widely by state, but they all have rules, and they're all written down. And there are unwritten rules. Let's consider an example of these unwritten rules in action.

In December 2018, New Yorker Jazmine Headley was arrested in the waiting room at the government food stamps office in Brooklyn. She was twenty-three, Black, and a new mother. The line at the food stamps office was long, and there were no chairs available, so Headley sat on the floor with her baby in her lap. She sat there for two hours. As a bonus irony, she was sitting in the area where families go for help in finding low-cost child-care. According to a report in the *New York Times*, "a female security guard eventually approached Ms. Headley, and several more guards followed as a verbal dispute escalated." A bystander, posting on Twitter, reported that the "security guard came over, said whatever she said to her and she made the security guard feel dumb, so she called the cops on her & this was the outcome. SMH. Mind you she had her baby in her hands the whole time."

Headley tried to explain her situation to the police, but they cut her off and laughed at her. The police asked Headley to come with them. Four police officers surrounded her, and video from bystanders shows that one "repeatedly yanks the child in an apparent attempt to separate him from his mother." One cop waved a stun gun around with her free hand, in a room full of impoverished New Yorkers, nearly all of them Black or Latinx. The police charged Jazmine Headley with resisting arrest, acting in a manner injurious to a child, obstructing governmental administration, and trespassing. They held her without bail on Rikers Island.[8]

Mothers of babies tend to attract empathy, but the power of empathy did not prevail at the food stamps office. The currencies of power that mattered were whiteness, a uniform, a baton, a gun, employment, and money. The power of financial self-reliance functioned here too: Headley's dependence on government benefits, like her Blackness, made her more vulnerable to the structural power of the authorities. The security guard and the police took advantage of their own official authority by gathering even more power: their possession of badges and guns entitled them to grab power that was not theirs to take. It is this terrifying effect of structural power that granted the officers the ability to yank the child and wave a gun in a crowded room.

Resources on Hand

Knowledge is power. Relationships, networks, and information are currencies of power. If a group has access to big data and the technical capacity to process it to elicit critical information, that group has power. But of all the knowledge a group in conflict may possess, the most valuable falls in two buckets: first, the skills required to navigate joint problem solving in Column A, and, second, the ability to mobilize power in Column B. These skills, which include negotiation, community organizing, mass protest, civil resistance, and military strategy, can tip the balance in a conflict where one group wields more structural power.

Of course, money is power too. Look at Figure 5.2: oil, gems, stock shares, and real estate are high-value currencies, whether individuals or the state own them. So are intellectual property rights and artistic talent. The brutal—but universally understood—potential of weapons is one of the most evident currencies of power. Both individuals and governments use the force of arms for revenge, punishment, and discipline and to attain whatever else they may need or want.

Governments do this through their police and militaries. The foundation of their power may be structural, but their arsenal consists of resources in the currencies of handcuffs, guns, and mortar rounds, along with the currencies of experience and skill with guns, Tasers, and choke holds. These resources amplify the strength inherent in the structural power of government agencies and their agents. If a person is suspected of violating a law, the government may use its resources to impose detainment, penalties, and punishments. If a person is found guilty or perceived as not cooperating with these state actions, they will be subject to successively harsher constraints, ultimately including imprisonment and physical force. Force backs up the authority of the state.

Much of what we think of as power is hurt or damage or the threat of hurt or damage. Threat is a distinct currency that may require a different amount of weaponry than you might need to actually damage people or property. One country may need a thousand nuclear weapons to deter a rival country from using its own nukes, but only two nukes to wipe that country out.[9]

At the same time, threat is a high-octane currency wielded effectively by both weaker and stronger parties. And weapons in the hands of the weak equalize power too.

Potential Power

Regardless of our net worth at birth, the schools we went to, or our natural athletic ability, every human being has capacities of intelligence, eagerness, and creativity in one form or another. We have unmet needs and aspirations that drive us. These capacities are the raw materials of potentially formidable power. They can be built or harnessed into impressive force, nonviolent or violent.

Potential power is the currency that democratizes power. You may not be powered-up in the structural currencies of credentials or a sense of white-skin entitlement, and you may not have a lot of money, much of a social network, advanced technical skills, or a gun, but you can still be loaded in terms of potential power. All around us are opportunities to transform freely available resources or opportunities into power. For example, if you don't have a gun, you can swing a baseball bat at someone or hit them over the head with a cast-iron frying pan. This necessitates a readiness to threaten and to harm, and functional upper arms, but it requires no ownership or access to expensive resources.

There is a science to the mobilization of potential power. There is theory, wisdom, morality, and discipline in the practices of community organizing, issue campaigning, nonviolent civil disobedience, and the mobilization of mass uprising. These, of course, are currencies of resource power, and they are useful in mobilizing potential power.

When groups combine the power of organizing people, strategic campaigning, mobilizing mass action, and building social movements, they make manifest the ultimate currency driven by human energy. This aggregated human energy is a currency that appears at first as only the potential for power, and then as mobilized power. In reality, however, the currency of human energy is the wealth that otherwise weak groups can develop to match the structural, economic, or military power of their opponents.

When the Philadelphia public access cable television activists protested, they were mobilizing their potential power. When they compared their power to the power of the city, they discovered their relative weakness in the present, just as the City of Seattle was at first less likely to get what it wanted than its opponent Amazon. The question in both instances was: "What is the balance of power at this stage of the conflict, with potential power not yet realized?"

Relative power changes. It is not surprising to find groups with weak negotiating positions choosing the power-building methods of Column B instead of the consensual methods of Column A, but when their currencies of power enable them to come to the table with BATNAs rivaling those of their adversaries, negotiation becomes their wisest course of action.

Since we are talking about the dynamics of the power of groups in a given moment, we need to hold the element of time in our focus. Our question for assessing relative power becomes: "If a negotiation were held now, which group would be more likely to get what it wants in the face of any obstacles controlled by the other?" If group Y holds more structural power and resources on hand than its opponent X in the present, then in the present Y is stronger. Group X may be brilliant at mobilizing potential power, but that requires action, progress, and time. In the present, Y is more powerful, and X would be wise to hold off on negotiating.

We can estimate a group's *potential power* by asking, "In the course of time, will the weaker party become as powerful as the currently stronger party?" By using the currencies of the weak, such as the ability to influence people, recruit members, plan strategic campaigns, mobilize movements, raise money, and elect candidates, the weaker party can become the stronger one.

When the weak orchestrate their currencies strategically over time, the power that results may not be permanent, but it can be so significant as to make it possible for the weaker group to get what it wants. This mobilization of potential power doesn't instantly become as entrenched, stable, or long-term as the power of the initially stronger group. Mobilized potential power does not necessarily become institutionalized.[10]

When group X successfully builds its power through mobilization, the power balance shifts. This puts group X in a position to negotiate with the opponent, which may be strong in institutionalized power but is now compelled to deal with the first group's demand. If the demand is more than a one-off need or desire, the weaker group may continue a dance between the strategies of negotiation and power building.

In the late 2010s, Facebook, for example, encountered popular anger about fair access to information and data privacy. In response to a well-organized campaign by consumers and grassroots activists, the tech giant committed to changing some of its practices. Media justice activist Malkia Devich Cyril described the inevitability of activists maintaining an ongoing Column A/B dance with Facebook: "While these short-term investments are critical, without long-term investments, these changes go to waste."[11] Facebook was put on notice that it would face a cycle of change; activists would mobilize power to compel the social media giant to negotiate. This would be followed by the activists' return to the streets to accrue more power and apply more pressure until a fundamental shift occurs in Facebook's institutionalized, structural power.

Gene Sharp laid out a guiding theory for weaker parties aiming to mobilize potential power. His focus was on the role of cooperation in maintaining the arrangements of structural power. When a weaker group recognizes that cooperation with the status quo is a choice and withdraws its cooperation, the stronger side's power loses traction. This was the theory behind the 1956 Montgomery bus boycott, and it was the principle behind the burning of draft cards by young men during the Vietnam War.[12]

Author and activist James Baldwin described a case of noncooperation in action during the 1960s. He was at a Nation of Islam demonstration, not as a participant but as an observer. As he watched the police refraining from their customary aggression against demonstrators, Baldwin observed:

[T]he policemen were doing nothing now. Obviously, this was not because they had become more human but because they were under orders and because they were afraid. And indeed they were, and I was delighted to see it. There they stood, in twos and threes and fours, in their Cub Scout uniforms and with their Cub Scout faces, totally unprepared, as is the way with American he-men, for anything that could not be settled with a club or a fist or a gun. I might have pitied them if I had not found myself in their hands so often and discovered, through ugly experience, what they were like when *they* held the power and what they were like when *you* held the power.[13]

The powerful expect the powerless to comply with their authority and abide by the rules. Our social arrangements do not equip a stronger group for a weaker group's noncompliance. For this reason, when a weaker group mobilizes its potential power against a stronger group, it may well be the stronger group that crumbles.

The principle of shifting from action within the constraints of social authority to initiative outside of those constraints is the basis for taking action in Column B or Column C. After all, Columns B and C, by definition, consist of nonconsensual activities for building power.

Lessons about Power

We have examined how power, manifesting in any of its many currencies, increases the ability of a group to remove obstacles placed by its opponents that prevent it from getting what it wants. Whether the opponents positioned these obstacles intentionally or not may have little bearing on the strategies that the first group must apply to remove them. Wisdom from the worlds of negotiation and social change suggest some additional realities about how groups in asymmetrical conflict interact.

Power dynamics are ubiquitous across organizations, communities, and society. Unbalanced power is ubiquitous in human systems. Every day, each one of us navigates power differences within our families, at schools and workplaces, in our mosques, synagogues, and churches, and in our neighborhoods. Government agencies and corporations set rules and obey unofficial practices that guide our economy and ensure that power is hard to shift. In every human setting, power is present, influencing social dynamics.

Power is ubiquitous inside groups. The currencies of power are present inside every human group. There are even power differences within groups explicitly committed to being egalitarian. Groups that profess a nonhierarchical structure may relegate their inevitable power dynamics to invisibility or secrecy, but they are present nonetheless.[14]

People seek power. People typically grow into adulthood with the knowledge that they ought to have power over decisions that affect them. This means that power differences—whether obvious, subtle, or invisible—are a significant factor in motivating action among weaker parties. These imbalances cause fistfights, family feuds, and wars.

Potential power is weak in Column A. In Column A, groups with more structural power and resources on hand are more likely to get what they want. But groups working only with potential power in Column A can threaten to mobilize their potential power. This is the power that a union exercises at the negotiating table when it threatens to strike if its demands are not met. The threat of mobilizing potential power, like any threat, is itself a type of resource power. The potential power gains strength when it is mobilized in Column B.

Unbalanced power affects perceptions of power. Groups in conflict are unlikely to agree on a definition of power, let alone on which group is more powerful. Unbalanced power relations have a profound impact on our self-perceived role in social systems and social struggles. The nature of relative powerlessness and the characteristics of the powerless tend to be imperceptible to the powerful; power protects the powerful from seeing beyond their reality. Because of this phenomenon, groups on different sides of a conflict have different perceptions of who has more power.

Power flows through families, organizations, communities, societies, and countries. Each of us creates a personal story of power as we comprehend it from our particular seat in our particular row of our particular theater. The more clearly we perceive the power of our group and of other groups, the more freedom, flexibility, and choice we have as we strategize to win.

CHAPTER 6

Structural Barriers

I know a thoughtful and lovely straight man, an Arab-American human rights advocate named Raed Jarrar. In 2006, Raed was detained by US airport authorities for having Arabic writing on his T-shirt.

As Raed made his way through the security line at JFK airport on his way to California, he was tapped for a secondary search. When that was done, he walked down to his gate. As he sat waiting for boarding to begin, two people with badges approached him, asked for his ID, and said, "People are offended by your T-shirt." Raed's T-shirt said, in both Arabic and English, "We will not be silent." The officials asked Raed if he had another shirt to change into. He didn't. He had checked his suitcase. To manage his growing aggravation, Raed asked, "Why do you want me to take off my T-shirt? Isn't it my constitutional right to express myself in this way?"

The officials said, "People here in the US don't understand these things about constitutional rights." Raed said, "I live in the US, and I understand it is my right to wear this T-shirt. I am prepared to change it if you tell me why I should." The man answered, "You can't wear a T-shirt with Arabic script and come to an airport. It's like wearing a shirt that reads 'I am a robber' and going to a bank." Raed said that the Arabic on his shirt had the same meaning as the English. The woman said he couldn't be sure of this, since there was no translator to confirm it. "Maybe it means something else."

They suggested that Raed turn his T-shirt inside-out, but he wouldn't. They offered to buy him a new T-shirt, but again he refused. They said, "We can't let you get on that airplane with your T-shirt. Let's end this the nice way." That was enough to make Raed feel threatened, so he said they could get him a new T-shirt. "Should we get you an 'I heart New York' T-shirt?"

said one, and the other answered, "No, we shouldn't ask him to go from one extreme to another." They came back with a gray T-shirt with the words "New York" blasted across the front.

Afterward, Raed commented on his post-9/11 airport experiences: "It sucks to be an Arab or Muslim living in the US these days. When you go to the Middle East, you are a US taxpayer destroying people's houses with your money, and when you come back to the US, you are a suspected terrorist hijacker."[1]

I do not share the experience of being thrust up against the structural barriers of race, or, for that matter, the race other people think you are, the racial identity you yourself carry, your perceived religion, your perceived social class. For me, at least in the coastal states and big cities where I spend most of my time, these barriers work in my favor. My whiteness and the speaking habits that betray my educational background land me on the right side of the biggest social barriers and allow me to maneuver with ease. I carry such a strong embedded sense of white middle-class entitlement that I invent ways to be detained at the airport. For instance, I have imagined making a T-shirt that says in Arabic, "What did you *think* it said?" Wouldn't that be something, I tell myself, to be taken aside because some passengers are concerned that it might say something terrible? For them to call in the FBI Arabic translator who would have to say, "uh, that T-shirt says, 'What did you *think* it said?'" What a hero I would be, taking a stand like that against Islamophobia and racism. Yet if I were Raed, I don't think that game would be amusing.

Here's my real-life story of Arabic at the airport. For years, my colleague Malek and I have worked together on assorted negotiation projects, including cofacilitation with Palestinian trainers on the West Bank. Several times in the mid-2000s, the two of us traveled together between the US and Tel Aviv. Malek is Palestinian-American, and his Arab heritage is easily recognizable by his last name too. In airports, Malek either worries about people mistaking him for an Israeli spy, or he's cautious about seeming offensive just by being his Arab self. One of his strategies for avoiding getting hassled is traveling in a Red Sox cap; he deliberately wears it to create the impression that he's the regular Boston guy that he actually is.

On our trips, airport officials would routinely ask Malek to step aside for extra screening. Israeli security officers would take him into a room and frisk him, and twice they kept his bags at the airport for days. I don't know what happened in the little room, but Malek, a Harvard-trained negotiator, has a strong Column A bias. We joke about it. I am certain that he used his de-escalation skills in that little room rather than show his anger.

Nevertheless, the two of us devised a Column B strategy for making this insult a bit easier on Malek. On our trips home through Tel Aviv, we would invariably have leftover training documents with English and Arabic writing. If we had lists of workshop participants, we discarded them before getting to the airport, but we would still have agendas and worksheets, brochures and souvenirs, bilingual booklets, menus, and maps in our bags. We would gather up Malek's Arabic papers and put them in my suitcase. At the first security checkpoint I would ask the official, "May I answer you in Hebrew?" "From where do you know Hebrew?" the young Israeli security guard would ask. "From Jewish school when I was younger." "Oh, very good for you. You know, your Hebrew is very good."

They would still tag Malek as potentially dangerous, but when they dumped out the contents of his suitcase into a messy heap, they found nothing of interest. They never gave my bags a second thought.

Structural Barriers

Structural barriers can be so formidable that they block weaker groups from following an effective strategy. Those structural barriers may be the root of the conflict in the first place. But even when groups are fighting over something more malleable, there may be structural barriers that limit them from making a claim for what they need or want. Raed and Malek just want to get on their planes and go home; they ask with courtesy, and though they may show or hide their anger, the decision about whether or not they will board is not up to them. The currencies of power that weaker parties hold are devalued, which leaves little space for building power; Column B action is out of the question. What can a weaker party do when faced with structural barriers?

Sometimes individuals and groups that cannot mobilize try to reach out to the stronger group, placing their hope in the possibility of listening, dialogue, and negotiation. Like a person deep in debt and pleading with the debt collector, it may be tempting to try to appeal to the stronger party's humanity. As you know, when the more powerful group is a lot more powerful, this doesn't usually work.

Have you heard of the ancient kingdom of Melos? Possibly not, because in 416 BCE the whole population of this small Greek island was destroyed by the army of Athens. This was during the Peloponnesian Wars, and the Athenians were on a roll. They sent a delegation to little Melos with a choice: submit to us as slaves, or we'll kill you all. The Melians tried to talk the Athenians out of it. You can guess what happened.

What could the Melians have done? What were their alternatives to negotiating with the Athenians? What could they have done unilaterally, without consent or buy-in from the Athenians? They could have submitted to slavery, tried to fight the Athenians off, or run to the hills. They could have reached out to the neighboring islands for backup. They could have committed mass suicide. Which was the least awful of these alternatives—that is, what was the Melians' BATNA? Was their best alternative to negotiate with the Athenians, who were asking the Melians to submit to slavery? Was dignity the most important value at play here, such that the Melians might have considered a futile fight, or even suicide, a better choice than submission?

We know from the historian Thucydides that the weaker Melians did indeed value their dignity most of all and saw negotiation as the most promising way to maintain their self-respect. "It were surely great baseness and cowardice in us who are still free not to try everything that can be tried, before submitting to your yoke," they said.[2] Yes, it can be tempting for a desperate weaker party to go to Column A to attempt to talk it out with an entrenched, much stronger power, but we can expect the weaker group to face the fate of the Melians.

Sometimes the weaker party chooses Column C action—in this case, fighting back, even with no hope of building power, in order to hurt the powerful group in any way possible. This is where we find a tenant writing "screw you" on the rent check or a frustrated accountholder stealing the bank's nice pens. Had the Melians started a fight with the Athenians, it would have been a good example of this type of futile Column C action. On the other hand, nonwinning Column C action isn't always futile. Stealing the pens or fighting the powerful can embolden members of a weaker group and boost their self-esteem. One-off disruptions that are not part of a strategic escalation by a weaker group have their place in the change-making repertoire. Acts of nonstrategic mischief, disruption, and terror, even when they play no direct part in a strategic mobilization, can increase fear and reduce the confidence of a stronger party. These actions can also attract the curious and build the ranks of a movement, improving the conditions for strategic mobilization.

Doing nothing is also an option for weaker people and groups facing structural power. It is important to pause on this "nothing" for a moment, because it is rarely truly nothing. If doing nothing means not acting in Column A, B, or C, it may mean just getting up in the morning. The song-writer Andra Day wrote about "rising unafraid." Getting up in the morning and surviving under the weight of a system so indomitable and severe that Column B activity is impossible isn't nothing. Acting polite when your boss is unfair, working three jobs when your neighbor earns three times as much working one—these are not good or just actions, but, in certain cases, they can lead to more wins in the medium- or long-term than thrashing about in distress. Resilient people live to fight another day.

You Can't Move a Boulder with a Fork

Let's stop to review the model. *Conflict* describes a situation in which one group wants something, but another group is in the way. When the power of the groups is balanced, we expect them to engage in Column A—joint consensual activity for the purpose of problem solving. On the other hand, if there is significant asymmetry of power, a weaker party would be more likely to mobilize its potential power to even out the disparity. This mobi-lization happens in Column B—unilateral nonconsensual activity for the purpose of building power, setting the stage to return to the joint problem solving of Column A. Sometimes a weaker party doesn't expect to ever get what it is fighting for from its opponents, either because of the nature of what it wants or because of the nature of its opposition. In that case, the only way to get what it wants is to overpower its rivals. This is Column C—unilateral nonconsensual activity for the purpose of vanquishing the opposition.

Power, structural barriers, principle, and biases are the primary factors in group decision-making about conflict strategy. We've consid-ered the three types of power: structural power, resources on hand, and potential power. We've considered how potential power can be mobilized against structural power and resource power. Next, I want to examine the barriers that may result from structural power and block the way for weaker parties to follow a strategy based on power.

You can follow along in the flowchart in Figure 6.1, if it helps you to see it laid out graphically.

The opening premise is that a group wants something that is blocked by another group, intentionally or not. The first group asks, "Do our rivals

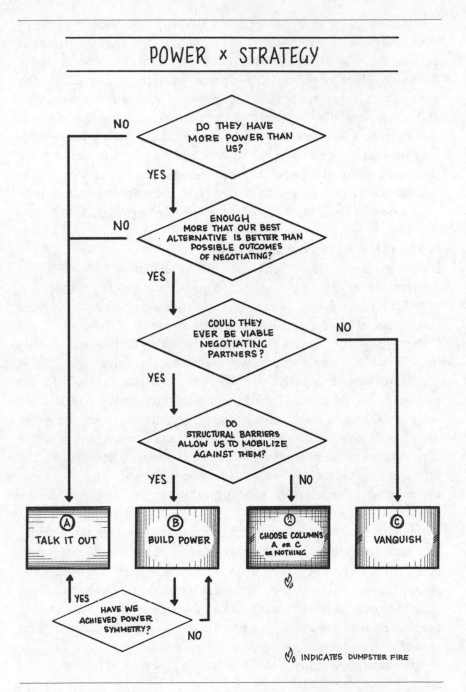

Figure 6.1: Power × strategy: a flow chart for analyzing a conflict in order to choose Column A, B, or C

have more power than we do?" If not—that is, if the power is balanced or if the opposition is weaker—the group goes to Column A to negotiate a solution with its opponents.

If the group's assessment is that their opponents are more powerful, they consider whether the opposition really has so much more power that their alternatives to negotiating are far better than what they can get by negotiating. Is it worth a fight? If not, then as in the first instance, the group takes a Column A, joint problem-solving approach.

If, on the other hand, the group has a solid yes—yes, the opposition is so much more powerful that we can't get what we need through negotiation—then they consider alternatives to Column A. First, the group considers whether or not their rivals consist of "viable negotiating partners." They consider whether or not, if power becomes balanced in the future, there would be any known reason why they couldn't work out something consensual with their opponents. Maybe the opposition is evil or unreachable for any useful negotiation like Hitler or Trump. Maybe the power of the opposition is self-perpetuating, built in, structural, like the fossil fuel industry, institutional racism, corporate capitalism, and patriarchy. These are strategically sound reasons for our protagonists to go to Column C.

If the group can imagine negotiating with their opponents in the event power becomes more balanced, they need to consider the question of structural barriers. Do structural barriers leave enough space for mobilizing power against the opposition? Or, as in Raed's case, do racism, Islamophobia, and the security forces that back up the power of airline officials allow their targets to mobilize power?

As the flow chart makes clear, a "no" to this question is what I call a "dumpster fire." Raed could choose to negotiate, a Column A approach, he could choose to punch the officials in the nose, a Column C approach, or he could choose to do nothing. He chose to negotiate, but, as we see, negotiating from a place of weakness yields subpar results. Unfortunately, the other two options might not have produced any better result in this case.

On the other hand, if our group in conflict is sufficiently free of structural barriers to executing a resistance strategy, they proceed to mobilize and win power. They conduct a strategic sequence of mobilizations, perhaps educating and organizing people, conducting campaigns, and building on opportunities for mass action. With every win, the group assesses the progress of their power building, asking, "Have we achieved power symmetry?" When they can finally answer "yes," it is time to sit down at the table with the opposition and rally their negotiating skills and strategy to negotiate the terms of a solution.

Know-and-Tell

As an observer, I am sometimes very judgmental of groups with guns. When a group of ethnic separatists blows up a train station or a kindergarten, I find it hard to accept their choice as a strategic inevitability. Can this possibly be a strategic choice? Is it an intentional Column C choice? Perhaps it is a logical progression from the structural barriers question when the answer is "no"—that is, structural barriers do not leave enough space to mobilize power against an opponent in Columns B or C. A group chooses not to submit to doomed negotiations in Column A or to the indignity of doing nothing. Instead, the group chooses to build power through a dumpster fire, metaphorical or not. They engage in acts of nonstrategic mischief, disruption, or terror, even acts as mild as stealing the bank's good pens. These acts do perform a function. Dumpster fire actions increase fear and reduce the confidence of the opposition, and they restore a sense of dignity to the group, while attracting the curious and building the ranks of a movement.

It is easy for me, as an observer, and for you, as a reader, to judge those whose choices don't match our own. One purpose of this book is to replace a reader's judgment of the strategic repertoires of others with an expansion of their own. Obviously, this involves an exploration of strategies other than their own. But these explorations are quite different when performed by stronger and weaker parties. Most of us find ourselves on the stronger side sometimes and on the weaker side at other times. When we are on the weaker side due to structural barriers, our choices are limited. But when we are stronger in the currencies of structural power, even though our choices are expansive, our perception of the dynamics of weakness may remain limited.

Therefore, for readers who frequently find themselves on the more powerful side of structural barriers, exploring the strategies of weaker groups involves the unveiling of the systems that prevent us from recognizing the other's strategies as rational. This is a rare exercise for more powerful individuals and groups, but it is essential to understanding conflict and systems of power.

We are talking here about how rank works in society; some groups have more power than others. We can describe these groups as "ranking" higher, while other groups rank lower. Much of society's attention, whether in politics and the economy or in mainstream media and culture, goes to "uprank" groups. People with better-paying jobs, white men, and people who conform to mainstream gender norms get a lot of prime-time viewing. This societal level of rank is evident to us all.

It is harder to perceive our own place as individuals within an organization, coalition, or society. All of us, whether as individuals or groups, perceive ourselves and our rank from our own points of view. When we find ourselves "downrank" in a given context, we have an additional layer of perception, a sixth sense. Downrank people and groups perceive themselves from their own points of view and also from what they perceive as the point of view of those uprank from them. As psychologist Susan Fiske wrote, "Attention follows power."[3] Groups that rank lower tend to "know" who's who and what's what uprank from them.

Fiske explained how these dynamics function among workers inside organizations. Her explanation can be applied to rank in communities and society as well:

> Because power is essentially control, people pay attention to those who have power. It is a simple principle: People pay attention to those who control their outcomes. In an effort to predict and possibly influence what is going to happen to them, people gather information about those with power. Consider the direction of attention in a large organization. Attention follows power. Attention is directed *up* the hierarchy. Secretaries know more about their bosses than vice versa; graduate students know more about their advisors than vice versa. Similar dynamics operate at convention social hours, as people cluster around those perceived to be powerful. Thus, the powerless are attentive to the powerful. By the same token, the powerful need not attend very much to those with less power, because less is at stake for the powerful with regard to their subordinates.[4]

Those uprank *need not* attend to the downrank. This is true for uprank faculty and downrank students, for citizens and undocumented immigrants, for descendants of European settlers and Indigenous Americans, and for wealthy and working people. It is true for white people and Black people.

Sociologist, historian, and activist W. E. B. Du Bois described this extra awareness by downrank groups as a double consciousness. People and groups facing structural barriers perceive reality from their own positions, of course, and to ensure their own ability to avoid violating the rules of structural power, downrank people develop a second perception of reality, as if from the perspective of those with stock in structural power. Speaking at the turn of the twentieth century, Du Bois observed that this second awareness is central to the experience of African Americans:

> [T]he Negro is a sort of seventh son, born with a veil, and gifted with second-sight in this American world,—a world which yields him no self-consciousness, but only lets him see himself through the revelation of the other world. It is a peculiar sensation, this double-consciousness, this sense of always looking at one's self through the eyes of others, of measuring one's soul by the tape of a world that looks on in amused contempt and pity.

Where an African American person has no choice but to see the world through through the eyes of others, it is the privilege of the white person to measure their worth through their own eyes.

> One feels his two-ness,—an American, a Negro; two souls, two thoughts, two unreconciled strivings; two warring ideals in one dark body, whose dogged strength alone keeps it from being torn asunder. The history of the American Negro is the history of this strife,—this longing to attain self-conscious manhood, to merge his double self into a better and truer self. In this merging he wishes neither of the older selves to be lost. He does not wish to Africanize America, for America has too much to teach the world and Africa; he does not wish to bleach his Negro blood in a flood of white Americanism, for he believes—foolishly, perhaps, but fervently—that Negro blood has yet a message for the world. He simply wishes to make it possible for a man to be both a Negro and an American without being cursed and spit upon by his fellows, without losing the opportunity of self-development.[5]

We learn from Du Bois that Black people, Brown people, immigrants, queers, and other "others" will need to expend energy if they are to think of themselves as primary examples of personhood and to author their own lives.

Powerful groups set the social and economic rules for downrank groups. Wherever a group falls in terms of rank, its members are in the position to "tell" those with less power how society will be organized and how decisions will be made. People in lower-ranking groups understand clearly how the rules get made and enforced.

Being part of uprank or downrank groups in society is not a choice. This ranking forms almost naturally, built on the history of society's economy, politics, and social norms. We know it even when we don't have a name for it. The stronger have more choices about the rules, and the weaker have extra perception about how those rules are made. You can see this dynamic represented by the know-and-tell model in Figure 6.2.

In organizations, stronger people and groups have more choices and more influence over the dynamics of rank and power. Here we are aided by titles and explicit hierarchies that function alongside the unnamed ones. In theory, this formal structure allows us to more readily set and enforce rules and norms that match our values about power and rank. However, even in a highly structured workplace, management holds the power of rule-making while holding an incomplete perception of the dynamics of lower-ranking workers. These imbalances of rank and perception make it difficult to change the structures of power in a workplace. When downrank groups try to get the rules changed, the rule makers, who are uprank, rarely hear their arguments, let alone make the changes. As in society at large, social structures and rules tend to stay as they are for a long time.

To attain more power, downrank groups may band together to get the attention of uprank groups. An uprank group typically perceives this as just noise or as a threat, at least at first. In society, uprank groups typically resist agitation by downrank groups until they find themselves forced or overpowered into changing. But in those organizations led by principled people with concern and motivation for equity and justice, change can happen by choice. When uprank people become aware of how the ranking system works and of their own previous ignorance about it, it becomes possible for them to develop more attention for downrank groups and make more room for them to speak and to exercise leadership. Eventually, together, they become able to shift how rank itself works.

The Injustice of Rank

We have probably all been part of a group, at least in school, where we riled each other up against a common "tyrant." Maybe we talked behind someone's back, perhaps the teacher's. In most workplaces, groups of employees have something to talk about when the boss steps away. In society, members of weaker groups support each other in the phases where structural power is too strong for the weaker group to mobilize. Despite an overwhelming imbalance of power, the weaker group can still experience episodes of healing, building hope, and the creation of cultures that support and inspire future resistance and change.

Whatever actions a weaker group may manage to take, existence in the shadow of entrenched structural power hurts people. Even if it provides

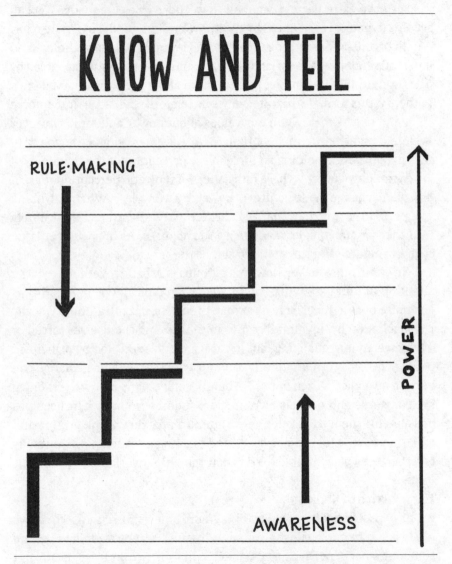

Figure 6.2: Know-and-tell: Downrank groups have the big view, but uprank groups make the rules.

opportunities for the internal strengthening of a group, it also damages the group and its members. The trauma of living under the boot of structural barriers affects the physical and psychological well-being of individual humans and the functionality and capacity of the groups we belong to. Even as weaker groups use lulls in mobilizing for self-care and life-sustaining community building, the trauma of an oppressive structure can breed a level of disempowerment that will have effects on the group's strategic choices in times of mobilization.

Within spaces of low power, where fighting would counter one's own interests and decrease rather than increase power, choices still exist, but they are extremely limited. It is the weaker party that perceives these dynamics, while the stronger party may not notice them.

When weaker groups mobilize successfully, they build power so strong that it balances the institutionalized power they face. As a result of this mobilization and the wins it generates, new circumstances, protections, and opportunities come into being on behalf of the weaker group.

In organizations, a win may mean that employees get higher wages and more vacation time, are subject to less disrespect and harassment, and have more say in how the workplace operates. In society, a win for people on the frontlines of danger may mean new access to food, money, education, housing, jobs, respect, freedom from incarceration, and dignity. Yet daily indignity, poverty, houselessness, ill health, criminalization, and alienation remain vast and persistent. Indigenous youth still have the highest school dropout rates, Black people are still incarcerated in alarmingly high numbers—six times the rate of white people—and income inequality is at an all-time high and rising.[6]

This isn't for lack of mobilizing. It's that some mountains are very, very high. For people who are Black, Latinx, poor, immigrants, trans, intellectually atypical, emotionally different, or, for that matter, fat, weak, old, underemployed, hard to understand, hard of hearing, physically abused, and/or in prison, mobilization short of revolution may not be a match for the most formidable mountains.

In 2014 and 2015, Black Lives Matter focused a bright light on state violence against Black people through its social media campaign, and that campaign propelled the Movement for Black Lives into prominence with the power of millions behind it. Yet this was insufficient to end structural or interpersonal racism. It isn't that it's impossible to mobilize and win significant gains; wins happen all the time. And there is no lack of ideas to implement; the Movement for Black Lives policy platform is full of them.[7] This movement succeeded in sparking a public conversation challenging this country to do for Black and Indigenous Americans what Germany did for Jews after World War II: offer reparations and conduct a serious and honest reckoning. We could make equality our top educational priority and our top legislative priority. There is no shortage of inquiries and articles describing what can be done.

As powerful as the Movement for Black Lives has been, and as impactful as the civil rights movement was before it, racism endures. It's fair to ask, what really is the point in fighting if the power gap between the weaker groups and the stronger is so vast? What if the barrier is just too high to scale? Then, just rising up out of bed every day becomes the triumph.

> You're broken down and tired
> Of living life on a merry go round
> And you can't find the fighter
> But. . .
> . . . I'll rise up
> And I'll do it a thousand times again
> —Andra Day, 2015[8]

I made rules for my kids when they were growing up, including: "Sit up in your chair at mealtimes"; "Do the dishes on your dish night"; "Don't say 'shut up' to your sibling." They knew those rules, because I said them. They also knew a lot of detail and subtlety about what would and wouldn't get them in trouble. All kids do.

At another extreme of authority, I recently watched an hour of webcam footage from a Mississippi state prison. Several men incarcerated at the prison had managed to get the video out to criminal justice activists in the hope that help might come to change their abysmal conditions. The camera took in a long row of chain-link cells, the webcam's microphone listened, and I watched, as men struggled to breathe through thickening smoke from a fire whose origin was beyond my sightlines. The prisoners were calling out for help; they couldn't get out of their cells. One man called out, "They will shoot to kill you, you know." It seemed the men had been abandoned and were desperate to escape the smoke.[9]

These men are locked up in ten-by-ten-foot cages for the very purpose of preventing them from doing what they wish. These men know the rules of that prison. They know the written rules, and they know what will cross a corrections officer. They know what will get them killed. There is no rule that says they will be shot if they do a particular thing, but they know it. The incarcerated men living on the outermost margins of power know better than their jailkeepers the unwritten rules of the prison.

I was struck recently by a bald public example of this kind of discrepancy between official and unarticulated rules. On Friday, January 5, 2020, bellicose exchanges between the Trump administration and the Iranian government began to peak. That night, dozens of Iranians and Iranian Americans tweeted that they were being detained, some for hours, at the US-Canadian border near Seattle. Many of them were returning from a concert by a popular Iranian performer. Some drove past the customs booths quietly with sleeping kids in their back seats. One tweeter said he thought he and his girlfriend had been stopped because their snow sports equipment was strewn in a heap across their back seat. When they went inside the customs building as asked, they recognized all the other people of Iranian heritage waiting there. Iranian American advocates and immigration activists retweeted these stories and demanded an explanation for the race-based detention of Americans and documented tourists.

On Saturday, January 6, the US Customs and Border Protection agency produced a statement: "Social media posts that CBP is detaining Iranian-Americans and refusing their entry into the US because of their country of origin are false. Reports that DHS/CBP has issued a related directive are also false."

By Saturday night, the *New York Times* and other mainstream media outlets had done their research and published the stories of more than sixty detentions of Iranians and Iranian Americans by the CBP.[10] In its blatant dishonesty about its actions, the government revealed the gap between what rule makers may say and what those with less power know to be the rules in force.

James Baldwin wrote, "Ask any Negro what he knows about the white people with whom he works. And then ask the white people with whom he works what they know about him."[11] The strong cannot perceive the currency of the weak, but the weak understand the currency of the strong quite clearly. Why don't white people know what structural barriers feel like to people of color? Because it is very difficult. It would require looking in the mirror, finding out things that we don't want to know, and, ultimately, losing aspects of our identities. Because it is difficult, white people do not do it unless we are required to, and we aren't. White people can get along just fine without knowing what our world looks like to people of color. Uprank people more generally can get along just fine without knowing what the world looks like to those downrank from them.

I think about whether or not I know the unspoken rules. It usually takes me a while to perceive them. Despite knowing that unspoken rules exist, I still retain a sense that the rules are explicit. No wonder; I grew up with so many explicit ones. I still assume it's all a big fair system, until I remember that it's not. Over and over and over again.

In *The Souls of Black Folk*, Du Bois described double consciousness as a replacement for the short-lived ease of childhood. He recalled the sweetness of early school years, playing games with both Black and white children. His is quite like a reflection on childhood from the white American poet William Wordsworth, in whose experience children come into the world with "heaven-born freedom":

> Heaven lies about us in our infancy!
> Shades of the prison-house begin to close
> Upon the growing Boy,
> But he beholds the light, and whence it flows,
> He sees it in his joy.[12]

That light of a common day grows out of reach for Du Bois. His earliest consciousness of his differentness, his Blackness, comes when a white child excludes him from a game. Du Bois learns the arbitrariness of the rules, wherein Black children grow into Black adults still at the mercy of rules they had no part in writing. As a white adult I don't perceive the arbitrary nature of the rules. I was taught that blue skies await me, await everyone, if we reach high enough. Du Bois learned from his exclusion that the walls are too high for the reach of a Black child:

> The shades of the prison-house closed round about us all: walls
> strait and stubborn to the whitest, but relentlessly narrow, tall, and
> unscalable to sons of night who must plod darkly against the stone,
> or steadily, half hopelessly watch the streak of blue above.[13]

That, I believe, is the power of our unbalanced culture. You can uncover your childhood traumas and your accumulated hurts and frustrations. You can make peace and make friends and make love. You can even win campaign after campaign. But overcoming the structures of power built into the greater culture and its institutions will take not only the mobilization of power but the mobilization of moral clarity.

Let's talk about that.

CHAPTER 7

Principle

Sometimes we are blessed with being able to choose the time and the arena and the manner of our revolution, but more usually we must do battle wherever we are standing.
—Audre Lorde[1]

This book is written for the reader who is interested in winning in a humane way. To you, neither the winning nor the humanity is dispensable. Our discussion of principle assumes that you believe that the actions we choose to help us make change must be humane. Strategy has to align with a set of values; social change requires principles.

At the same time, our understanding of "humane" must reckon with the limitations of structural barriers. Racism, sexism, and ableism constrict the ability of downrank people to center principle in a strategy for change. We all must do battle where we are standing, and while we can't always select our ideal course of action, we always face some element of choice, however subtle.

Imagine the challenges faced in the 1950s by civil rights activists in the South who wanted to abolish the web of anti-Black and anti-Indian laws that had persisted since Reconstruction. They faced not only the barriers of laws and culture but also the self-perpetuating system that included institutions, attitudes, public budgets, public buildings, and a million overlapping threads woven through Southern society. Writing in 1960, a *New York Times* reporter described Birmingham this way: "Every channel of communication, every medium of mutual interest, every reasoned approach, every inch of middle ground has been fragmented by the emotional dynamite of racism, enforced by the whip, the razor, the gun, the bomb, the torch, the club, the knife, the mob, the police and many branches of the state's apparatus." These overlapping racist arrangements formed a structural barrier that limited a group's choices of how to approach the struggle.[2]

Still, the civil rights activists stood in a place of allegiance to humanity. Some civil rights groups took part in Column A deal-making when they had mobilized sufficient power to force their opponents to take them seriously. Some groups mobilized in Column B, building the power that made negotiation possible, and others mobilized in Column C, fighting to dismantle the underlying structural barriers themselves. The activists' choices were based on their best strategic thinking, as well as on a sense of what was right.

Theorist and activist Saul Alinsky taught that the viability of questions of ethics in social struggle is relative. He wrote that "Life is a corrupting process from the time a child learns to play his mother off against his father in the politics of when to go to bed; he who fears corruption fears life."[3] To Alinsky, questions of principle may not even have been essential to Gandhi's powerful strategy of nonviolent disobedience: "the 'morality' which surrounded [Gandhi's] policy of passive resistance was to a large degree a rationale to cloak a pragmatic program with a desired and essential moral cover."[4]

The answers are relative, sure, but I disagree with Alinsky; the questions are always viable. Just because our own answers differ from situation to situation in questions of principle, that doesn't mean that our principles are not important. There are always choices for us to make, decisions about whether or not to go limp or tighten our muscles, whether or not to try fighting, whether or not to die fighting.

My own values are reflected in the theory, examples, and stories I have chosen to share in this book. I would bet that you have identified places where your values differ from mine. I rank humane behavior over life, and life over the vanity of ethical consistency. Your values and mine need not be the same. It is essential, though, to know what principles you are working with. This chapter will focus on the role of values in a group's choice of approach to conflict. It won't focus on the ethics of tactics but, rather, on the ethics of overall approaches to the question of whether to talk or to fight.

The question of talking vs. fighting is embedded in every social struggle, every drive for workplace change, and every neighborhood campaign. In the social change-related conflicts you have cared about, have you backed talkers, fighters, or both? Have you been both? The white women's rights campaigner Elizabeth Cady Stanton opposed the 15th Amendment, because it gave Black men the vote before any women had the franchise. Would you have supported the 15th Amendment or held out for universal suffrage? The 1980s feminist activist Andrea Dworkin organized against pornography together with conservative Christian opponents of pornography.[5] Would you join a coalition that includes a group that espouses things you oppose? Would you have negotiated with Senator Joe McCarthy?

Any group of workers, organizers, political activists, changemakers, community builders, or rebels deals with questions like these. In answering them, groups evaluate power dynamics. They also consider the structural barriers that constrict the universe of possible approaches. We have covered those two topics in previous chapters. But there are two more key factors in group decisions on whether to talk or to fight: these are the *principles* that guide our choices, as well as the *biases and inclinations* that steer us either toward talking or toward fighting. Either factor may function without a lot of conscious attention.

We will get deeper into biases in chapter 8, but, in the meantime, our biases will show up in discussing principle. Our values themselves bias us toward certain methods and away from others. For example, Gene Sharp pounded on the table when discussing the *strategic* value of nonviolent civil disobedience to distance himself from strictly *moral* justifications for avoiding violence in movements for social change. In so doing, he separated himself from his pacifist past, and the stridency with which he did so suggested a convert's zeal. Ironically, it's not at all unusual for changemakers to act this way, trying to avoid any appearance of assessing strategy choices through a moral lens. Yes, often changemakers are conscious of the role of principle in our conflict strategy; ethical dilemmas are the focus of many a strategy session. But, at other times, we may steer away from sounding as if we were driven by concern that social change be conducted humanely, even when our approach is altogether humane.

I think of strategy and values as twin inputs to strategy making. Power and principle both help steer our way through conflict. The principled strategist uses three special ethics tools that we will map out in this chapter. The first is the assessment of means and ends, or whether or not a method is ethically suitable to meet a particular problem. The second is the question of last resort, which functions in social conflict as it does in questions of war and peace: Have we exhausted the approaches to conflict, narrowing our options to one inevitability, even if the sole remaining option is distasteful? The third is the idea of having a values test—a set of criteria that a group uses to evaluate any strategy. These three tools help changemakers to connect power and principle in making strategy choices. Studying them will help us to connect power with principle in conflict strategy.

Means and Ends

Merriam-Webster defines *humane* as "marked by compassion, sympathy, or consideration for humans." If humanity isn't at the center of our work for equity, dignity, freedom, or justice, what's the point in trying to make the world more habitable for people? This question is a real challenge in a discussion that takes as its starting point the legitimacy of both talking and fighting. Talking with a contemptable opponent may violate the humanity of people we care about. On the other hand, some people may feel that fighting, in any form, is a violation of the humanity of those against whom we fight, as well as a violation of our own humanity.

It is possible for a group to be so concerned with acting virtuously that it winds up more focused on the purity of its methods than on the achievement of its goals. At another extreme, a group with humane goals may follow what you consider to be an inhumane changemaking strategy. Perhaps the group believes that a principled goal justifies unprincipled action. It may not believe its action is unprincipled; it may believe the humanity of an action is relative. While the merit of the goal doesn't provide a blanket justification for every imaginable action, to such a group, context is the primary factor in evaluating whether or not the method is suitably humane in any given case.

Is any activity as worthy as the result we are using it to achieve? In other words, do worthy ends justify every possible means?

According to Saul Alinsky, a righteous end justifies any means of achieving it. In the second chapter of *Rules for Radicals*, Alinsky dismembered the ethical relationship between means and ends. He wrote, "You do what you can with what you have and clothe it with moral garments." His argument was grounded in his experience of power asymmetries: "As an organizer I start from where the world is, as it is, not as I would like it to be. That we accept the world as it is does not in any sense weaken our desire to change it into what we believe it should be—it is necessary to begin where the world is if we are going to change it to what we think it should be." Sure enough, his characterizations of strategy are void of the morality that moves him in the first place. Alinsky views means and ends with a morally prescriptive realism: in order to shift power to the people—the only righteous end—strategists must view their fight dispassionately, because the corporations and governments they have to fight against don't subject *their* strategies to any moral review.[6]

I don't believe that a legitimate end justifies the entire universe of possible means. But there are cases where a particular end justifies a particular means. For twenty semesters, I taught an introductory peace and conflict course to undergraduates. In our first session, I would lead an exercise in which the students placed themselves along an imaginary line representing the spectrum of views on killing. I would ask, "Is it ever acceptable to kill someone?" There were typically thirty-five students in a class, including one or two pacifists and a couple of Ayn Rand fans. In between, there would be an even spread of students who thought it was acceptable to kill in self-defense or in the defense of others, students who weren't sure, and students who doubted that it was ever acceptable to kill but weren't prepared to say "never."

One of the most challenging dilemmas in the discussion that followed that exercise was grappling with the three possible propositions about killing: sometimes you will kill; sometimes you must kill; sometimes it is right to kill. "Sometimes you will kill" is a realist's perspective, an acknowledgment that humans, acting in our own self-interest, are bound to do troubling things, and that it is unrealistic to expect ourselves to prioritize the interests of others instinctively. During the French-Algerian war, the writer Albert Camus was quoted as saying, "I believe in justice, but I will defend my mother before justice."[7] That is what we humans do.

Ethicists will continue to debate whether or not you must kill in some instances, and whether or not it is ever right to kill. But surely there are more and less humane choices in a given circumstance. What is certainly wrong is not to consider humanity as a factor in making the decision. A just model of conflict must recognize that neither the achievement of a righteous goal nor the humanity with which we seek to attain it is dispensable.

Last Resort

In talking about conflict, we are accustomed to posing the question of humanity in terms of violence. You may have noticed that violence hasn't featured in this discussion much. In fact, I have grouped nonviolent confrontation and armed resistance together in both Column B and Column C.

The model explored in this book reduces the distinction between violent and nonviolent activity from the primary position it typically holds in questions of conflict management to its place as one of many tensions inherent in conflict. The question of whether or not to use force is secondary to the first-order question of whether or not to engage an opponent in Column A, B, or C—whether to talk or to fight, and if the decision is to fight, whether to fight to build power or to vanquish the opposition.

Before we dismiss violence as a topic in the question of whether to talk or to fight, let's use it as an example for considering the question of means and ends. In his 1964 "The Ballot or the Bullet" speech, Malcolm X suggested that any method, even violence, is legitimate when the goals are important enough. He stated:

> I believe in action on all fronts by whatever means necessary.... We will work with anybody, anywhere, at any time, who is genuinely interested in tackling the problem head-on, nonviolently as long as the enemy is nonviolent, but violent when the enemy gets violent.[8]

Malcolm described two ethical characteristics of the use of violence. First, its use is justified by its use by one's opponent. Second, it is not warranted unless or until a certain point in time—the point at which the opponent uses violence. If and when the enemy gets violent, violence will be warranted.

To Malcolm, the use of violence is a *last resort*. In the first instance, it is not acceptable. If and when other methods of achieving a goal are ruled out, violence becomes acceptable. It is a method of last resort. The assumption in the expression "last resort" is that we prefer a less destructive course to one that is more so, and, therefore, we limit the use of the more destructive course. This is the case whether we're defining the time to use violence, the time to protest, or the time to use a particular type of lethal weapon.

When it is possible to win using a joint approach to the resolution of a conflict, it is essential to use a joint approach. I would go further: when it is possible to win coming from a place of compassion, it is necessary to come from a place of compassion. An approach devoid of compassion is acceptable only when a compassionate approach is insufficient. Sometimes, it is not possible to achieve a goal using joint approaches. In this case, using a joint approach is not humane, even though it may seem to be compassionate. And if your workplace or political community considers nonconsensual action to be unacceptable under any circumstances, this bias against ever abandoning a Column A approach militates against good strategy.

The mechanism of designating a certain approach as a last resort infuses strategy with the compassion that defines our humanity. The sharpness of strategy can seem antithetical to compassion, but the practice of keeping a last resort in mind shows us that this is not so. With a last resort mapped out as a guide to our choice at every stage, strategy maximizes compassion by locating the most humane workable approach to winning.

Consider an action that you believe is unacceptable except under certain circumstances. Under those certain circumstances, that action becomes acceptable, because it is necessary, and there is no substitute. It is not optional. It is the last resort.

The last resort is one alternative among many. We want to limit the use of this awful thing; this option is marginal, bad, least preferred, and will be chosen only if there is no other way. In time, it may become the only available choice. Then we will do it, not because we want to, but because there is no alternative. Ergo, not only may we do it—we *must* do it. There is no alternative.

What makes the last resort unique is that we are committed to avoiding it unless it is our sole remaining alternative. If and when it is our sole remaining alternative, it is the option we will choose. We identified it early on as a viable, if least preferred, option, but when circumstances eliminate the alternatives, the last resort becomes the one viable way forward.

Borrowing from the Ethics of War

According to the widely studied just war doctrine, war is morally acceptable only after a country or countries have exhausted all peaceful options. While some of us think war is a viable last resort in disputes among nations, others will emphasize that it is always possible to find an alternative to physical violence. Most pacifists will say that, regardless of what alternatives may exist, war is never acceptable. On the other hand, to realists, war is a question of practicality rather than morality.

War involves its own strategic considerations, but in the dynamic between talking and fighting, it is much like social conflict. Former national security advisor Henry Kissinger modeled a brilliant if immoral and ruthless approach to international relations (as well as pre-#MeToo misogyny). But clear as a bell at age ninety-three, Kissinger described the choice countries make between diplomacy and force:

> The use of force is the ultimate sanction of diplomacy. Diplomacy and power are not discrete activities. They are linked, though not in the sense that each time negotiations stall, you resort to force. It simply means that the opposite number in a negotiation needs to know there is a breaking point at which you will attempt to impose your will. Otherwise, there will be a deadlock or a diplomatic defeat. That point is dependent on three components: the possession of adequate and relevant power, tactical willingness to deploy it, and a strategic doctrine that disciplines a society's power with its values.[9]

Studying the ethics of last resort in the context of war can help us understand fighting as a last resort in social conflict. The flow chart in Figure 7.1 lays out questions of whether or not and under what circumstances it may be acceptable for a country to go to war.

If you, like Kissinger, are a realist, you will scramble down to the lower right for a cost-benefit analysis to determine whether or not to go to war. If you are a pacifist, you will land on "don't go to war." If you understand the question as a moral one based on several factors, you will ask yourselves a series of questions to determine whether or not to choose war.

Inside the moral question of whether or not to choose war, you may care deeply about avoiding war, in which case you will find yourself in the shaded loop on the lower left, exploring alternatives to war until you're at the point of last resort. How will you know you are at that point? You won't ever be able to know for certain. You can just make a real-world decision about when you have exhausted the alternatives.

In chapter 2, we read of Dr. King's frustration with the white moderate "who is more devoted to 'order' than to justice; who prefers a negative peace which is the absence of tension to a positive peace which is the presence of justice; who constantly says 'I agree with you in the goal you seek, but I can't agree with your methods of direct action'; who paternalistically feels he can set the timetable for another man's freedom; who lives by the myth of time and who constantly advises the Negro to wait until a 'more convenient season.'"[10] Dr. King is referring to those who admonish civil rights advocates not to go to Column B. When is it time to employ the last resort? How long do you go on with labor negotiations when your employer is clearly stalling for time? At what moment are you truly "sick

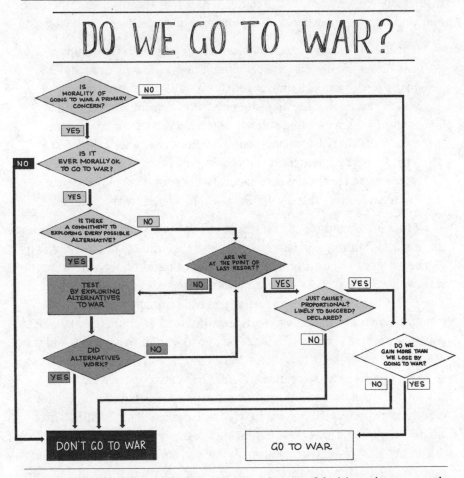

DO WE GO TO WAR?

Figure 7.1: Do we go to war? Last resort is a key element of decisions about war and peace.

and tired and not going to take it anymore?" These are not easily measurable. Theoretically one could always generate more potential alternatives. But when you can't come up with any more credible ones, and the moment becomes desperate, you will sense that it is time for the last resort.

Dr. King's comrade Ralph Abernathy said in 1963: "They say this is the wrong time and yet they have had 350 years. I want to know when the devil gives the right time."[11]

What we do know is that there is a time to talk and a time to fight. Power dynamics help us to choose, and structural barriers can limit our choices. Principle helps us to know which approaches are always unacceptable and which are reserved for our last resort. Though it may be an insufficiently precise measure for some, our own discernment enables us to know when the time for last resort has arrived.

A Values Test

To make difficult decisions in real time, you need to plan ahead. To make strategic decisions about whether or not to problem solve in Column A, build power in Column B, or vanquish an opponent in Column C, groups do well to have an established set of criteria to match their closely held values and principles.

This is not to say what principles are acceptable. It is to argue that you should know what is acceptable to yourself, on principle, before you determine your strategy or action. In other words, people who want to change the world ought to practice aligning their actions with their values. That's the only way to credibly claim that your strategy is "just," "fair," or "legitimate," regardless of your definition of justice or fairness or morality.

A group must have some kind of evaluation method as a way to apply its principles to a strategy. Figure 7.2 shows an example of a principle

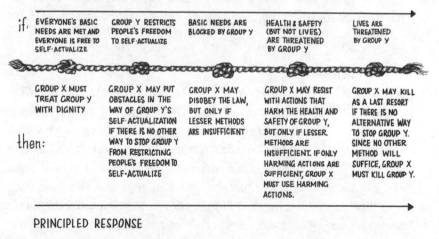

EXAMPLE OF A PRINCIPLE SCREEN

NEED THREATENED

if:

| EVERYONE'S BASIC NEEDS ARE MET AND EVERYONE IS FREE TO SELF-ACTUALIZE | GROUP Y RESTRICTS PEOPLE'S FREEDOM TO SELF-ACTUALIZE | BASIC NEEDS ARE BLOCKED BY GROUP Y | HEALTH & SAFETY (BUT NOT LIVES) ARE THREATENED BY GROUP Y | LIVES ARE THREATENED BY GROUP Y |

then:

| GROUP X MUST TREAT GROUP Y WITH DIGNITY | GROUP X MAY PUT OBSTACLES IN THE WAY OF GROUP Y'S SELF-ACTUALIZATION IF THERE IS NO OTHER WAY TO STOP GROUP Y FROM RESTRICTING PEOPLE'S FREEDOM TO SELF-ACTUALIZE | GROUP X MAY DISOBEY THE LAW, BUT ONLY IF LESSER METHODS ARE INSUFFICIENT | GROUP X MAY RESIST WITH ACTIONS THAT HARM THE HEALTH AND SAFETY OF GROUP Y, BUT ONLY IF LESSER METHODS ARE INSUFFICIENT. IF ONLY HARMING ACTIONS ARE SUFFICIENT, GROUP X MUST USE HARMING ACTIONS. | GROUP X MAY KILL AS A LAST RESORT IF THERE IS NO ALTERNATIVE WAY TO STOP GROUP Y. SINCE NO OTHER METHOD WILL SUFFICE, GROUP X MUST KILL GROUP Y. |

PRINCIPLED RESPONSE

Figure 7.2: Example of a principle screen as one type of values test; based in part on Abraham Maslow's hierarchy of needs

screen—a tool for a group to use in testing a possible strategy against its values. The principle screen builds on the frames of means and ends and last resort and on the principle of proportionality, another principle of war ethics. The values test shown here is based on the principles that any group X has the right to expect any group Y not to obstruct access to its needs and desires; and that if group Y gets in group X's way, group X will limit its response in line with its ethical considerations. The tool shows scenarios for a set of hypothetical violations by group Y and proportional responses from group X.

Figure 7.2 specifies the most severe appropriate response for each scenario. In each case, the most severe response would be appropriate if and only if there were no less severe responses available. Such a situation leaves a group with two options: the one listed or suffering from the unmet need.

This values test reflects the values and beliefs of the group that created it and has implications for the group in choosing its approach to conflict. On the far-left side, group Y is not obstructing group X's ability to get its basic needs met, and group X believes it must negotiate or jointly problem solve whatever conflict exists between the two groups. The next two situations suggest a Column B campaign to mobilize power. Further to the right are Column C scenarios.

We don't all share the same values and moral commitments, but we all have some. These matter in our decisions. A group needs practical standards against which to assess its adherence to particular methods, under particular circumstances, and to connect those methods to the group's values and principles.

Principle and Bias

In his chilling opus on Stalin's Russia, Aleksandr Solzhenitsyn considers the prosaic and arbitrary nature of our choices of when to act: "At what exact point, then, should one resist? When one's belt is taken away? When one is ordered to face into a corner? When one crosses the threshold of one's home? An arrest consists of a series of incidental irrelevancies, of a multitude of things that do not matter."[12] Our judgments about what ends justify which means are inevitably tainted by our roles and our points of view. Our discernment about whether or not we have arrived at the moment of last resort is affected by our emotions and inclinations. Our evaluation of a potential action against our values is shaped by habits and social forces.

In short, a group's choices of whether, when, and how to resist and whether, when, and how to talk are shaped by factors apart from strategy and principle. It is easy to lose track of principle, just as it is hard to make choices consistent with the rational path of strategy. Our biases obscure our own perception of principle, just as they obscure a hard analysis of strategy. That is precisely why we'll consider biases next.

CHAPTER 8

Biases

Someday we'll find it, the rainbow connection,
The lovers, the dreamers and me.
—The Muppets[1]

I'm a very direct woman. If I do not get that approval—and please
understand that I have a controlling interest in Denver-Carrington—I
shall fire you all on the spot and replace you with a board that will
approve of the merger.
—Alexis Carrington on *Dynasty*[2]

My Three Hates

For some people, the bluntness of Alexis on *Dynasty* is a relief; she's willing
to exercise power without remorse. Others will find it easier to relate to
the Muppets with their reliable drive toward mutual understanding and
connection. I am going to go hard on both Alexis and the Muppets in this
chapter, by which I mean that I will be very tough with both dialogue
groups and resistance groups. After all, the main purposes of this book
are to light a fire under people who would bring the world's best possible
negotiation game to a fight with a power delta gaping so wide that negotiations are doomed until they build enough power to match their opponents
and to shake up truly badass activists who don't know how to make a deal
once they've won the power to sit at the table.

My ex Julie raised five kids with a rule about food choices. You could
hate three foods at a time, and each kid's "hate" list was stuck to the fridge.
You could switch them around, but at any given moment you could refuse
to eat a maximum of three foods. I must have internalized the rule, because

I carry around three very strong hates. If I were to count my hated foods there would be more than three: rhubarb, sriracha, olives, blue cheese, and pickled anything but pickles. But sociopolitically speaking, I have three big hates (not counting things like murder, hunger, slavery, oppression, and cancer).

First, I hate it when people say they're doing something for a strategic reason, when it's actually a matter of principle for them. Your belief in what is right and necessary is a powerful force, not something to be hidden or wasted! I flipped my life upside-down over the difference between my moral stand and that of my parents, my family, and my community. Principles are good. Discerning how you think the world could be fairer is good. I hate it when people hide goodness to seem cool.

Second, I hate it when people are unkind to each other, because they think it's corny to appear weak. Kindness isn't corny or weak; it's necessary for living, and it is, therefore, urgent.

Third, I hate it when people are too afraid to fight. This includes fellow Jews who would rather have dialogue with Palestinians than take action to change the power dynamics of the conflict and fellow white people who want to end racism through dialogue with Black people instead of confronting white supremacy. Get a spine!

Keeping biases from trumping strategy and principle requires difficult personal work. It may be optional to spend time understanding one's own biases outside the context of conflict, but when someone else is holding onto something you need, the stakes are high. Inside a conflict, it is essential to understand the biases and inclinations of the different parties involved. You need to know what motivates and influences each group, their habits, and their assumptions. To achieve all that, you and your group need to raise your own awareness of some of the subtler elements of the conflict dynamic.

Turtles

I need to get a spine myself. No one is unbiased, and I'm not the exception. One morning during a book-writing retreat, I paddled across Lake Owassa through the morning wind to the labyrinth of shallow streams that wind through Bear Swamp Wildlife Management Area, near the Delaware Water Gap. In the swamp, I saw seven silvery turtles sunning themselves on moss, and each, as they sensed my admiration, plopped into the lagoon. As the wind pushed me back toward the lake, it got hot, so I took off my hoodie—but not completely off. I left it hanging around my neck, because underneath I was wearing my "Palestinians Should Be Free" T-shirt. On the back of the T-shirt is a checklist of causes: climate justice, Black Lives Matter, fighting anti-Muslim hate, universal health care, debt-free education, open borders, livable wage. At the bottom was "Jewish Voice for Peace," in a small font, .org, so a person could order their own.

With the shore of Lake Owassa lined with American flags, I know it wasn't convenience alone that made me leave my hoodie around my neck like a muffler. The sun wasn't fully out, and the breeze justified a bit of a second layer, but there was more going on for me. In the back of my mind I was carrying the idea that this gender I wear and the politics around it could make me the target of danger. Rationally, this was a bit suspect: Danger? Really, in North Jersey in the summer of 2019? Danger of judgment, certainly. To be fair, I was already on alert for bears. I'm not sure I was measuring danger accurately. But I have the emotional habits of an old butch. My transgender younger child calls them vintage feelings; they feed on the embers of dying structural barriers.

A woman waved from behind a family's dock, all smiley with kids running around. I waved back. I was happy to be recognized as a fellow human being. She could see that I was white. I wanted to hide everything that made me not the type of white I assumed she was. Assumed! Type of white! Didn't want to be myself! Under my day-to-day confidence and cocky extroversion there lies a racist scaredy-cat ready to pounce on anyone who doesn't like who I am—but just as ready to hide. I am always ready to fight, and I am just as likely to retreat into my hoodie.

Another Explanation: Being of the Desert Generation

Metaphorically speaking, I am of the *dor hamidbar*, the generation of the desert, the Israelites who spent the book of Exodus wandering from Egypt toward ancient Palestine. The Jews who walked the desert for forty years didn't get to enter the promised land. The baggage of Egypt and slavery left them unequipped for settled life.

Most people I know are from the desert generation. There are queers who, like me, came out before coming out became easier in big-city America, and we are forever outsiders, even though today *Vogue* shows trans people as models. There are Jews. There are African Americans, grandchildren of housecleaners, who have earned degrees from Berkeley or Brown. There is the immigrant court translator who grew up interpreting English for their parents. They're new around here, as I am, and maybe you are too. Even though thirty-five years have passed since I came out as all the things I am, I still don't feel confident that I'll be accepted. I'm never sure I'm holding my fork right.

My kids, it turns out, can't enter the promised land either. They are second-generation desert people. They are "queerspawn" and "second gen queers"; that extra generation still didn't bring them all the way across the river. One generation down, they still carry some of the trauma of an immigrant heritage, and, unlike me, they are the children of a cultural refugee.

In the story, the original desert Jews cried, "Take us back to Egypt! Better to die there than camp with scorpions." If we carry the scars of old scorpion bites, we carry trauma. The trauma of the old bites makes the new ones sting even worse.

Yesterday, I was on a call with my siblings. "Where you going to stay when you go to Jerusalem next month?" I'm going there to visit my dad and stepmom. My brother recommended an Airbnb where he had stayed. "Let me know if you want the info. It was really convenient." "Not sure, I'll probably stay in the place I stayed at a couple years ago. The place in East Jerusalem." Because I can put my jeans back on and walk through the lobby like a person. Because Arabs are human there. Because I can stop censoring my politics.

I heard my partner, Barbary, describe for a friend the trip we took together to Jerusalem and Ramallah: "I got whiplash. In Ramallah we could be ourselves, but Rebecca didn't feel okay about outing us as partners; it seemed disrespectful. Same thing at her dad's, we could talk about everything, like queerness. Not that they feel good about it, but Bec had gone through all that revealing over the years. But we couldn't talk about the demonstration we'd just come from at the Gaza border."

Maybe we can measure the weight of our individual trauma collections and the pinches and punches of the present ones by the time we have spent downrank, worrying about credit, food, and guns, experiencing indignity and failing to achieve, and by the trauma collections of those who raised us. Trauma might be why we do anything irrational. When the stakes are high, the scars on our old hurt places tremble. Yet when the stakes are high it is important to think through the ways what we choose now may influence the future.

If you have touched bottom or spent time in a consequentially down-rank place, you have had a dog's-eye view of how power works. You have developed an ear for its pitch; you can hear what the uprank miss entirely. You perceive the rule-making apparatus from its underside. You know what's uprank, and the uprank make the rules for you. Your perception of the arrangements is clear as a bell, but your ability to make your will manifest is shaky; you feel powerless. This is not just because you are missing resources or facing structural barriers; it's also because you have sensitive scars. When an old wound is open, it can take tremendous willpower to push through feelings of helplessness in order to think through the future consequences of our present decisions.

All of these past traumas and experiences contribute to our biases. They affect how we choose to act when conflict rears its head. We might think we are acting in the moment, but it may be the old experience at the bottom that's actually doing the deciding.

For uprank and downrank people alike, family-of-origin dynamics and other childhood experiences, such as socioeconomic class, racial identity, neighborhood, and gender experience contribute to the development of our biases. These biases affect our cognition, our judgment, our attitudes, and our emotions. Our biases are influenced along the way by books, school, friends, media, and popular culture. They may develop out of the culture's response to the bodies we were born with, and they are affected by the support and resources available to us as we experience challenges and joys. The experiences from which our biases emerge may be more or less traumatic. It's obvious how biases in our thinking result from cognitive, social, emotional, and physical experiences. Our individual biases emerge from the social forces, social norms, and social pressures around us. All of these biases, in turn, influence our response to the values and behaviors we encounter in others and in ourselves, and they also influence our response to conflict itself.[3]

Consider your instincts around difficult decisions in conflicts. If you saw pamphlets you strongly opposed at the Attica Brothers Legal Defense offices, as I did when I was a kid, would you steal them? To raise the negotiating power of Palestinians against Israel, would you boycott Israeli goods? If you worked at Amazon, would you steal the merchandise? Would you take down a caricature of a minstrel in blackface that you found framed on the wall at an Airbnb? If you did, would you put it back before you left? Or would you throw it out? If you had the chance, would you punch a Nazi? Would you invite the Nazi out for a drink to connect across your differences? Set up a dialogue? Set aside the past and compromise on a future that everyone can live with?

You may have an instinct about which of these you would do, independent of questions of power, barriers, and principle. Our biases can exert considerable force on our decision-making. Maybe we want to belong more than we want to win, or we feel an urge to flex our power. We like the people who fight, so we go and fight too, or we fight because we have a strong political or cultural identity as fighters. We may think of ourselves as lovers and not fighters. A fear of fights may draw us again and again to dialogue. The time we have invested in learning negotiation skills may predispose us to negotiation. A well of anger may lead us to a constant fighting stance.

We are drawn to groups made up of people with inclinations like our own. Working together, socializing, and taking political action together help to develop a group's common inclinations and biases toward either talking or fighting as approaches to making change. But if you want to win, rather than allowing your biases to lead you, these important choices should involve an assessment of power relations, clarity about principles, and an awareness that structural barriers may constrict you and prevent you from doing what would otherwise be your strategic and ethical choice. The more aware we as people and groups are of our biases, the more strategically we play our parts.

Group Biases

Optimally, groups facing social conflict search for a principled path through Columns A, B, and C that will lead to winning efficiently. But most groups start with a favorite path. When Donald Trump first became president, some groups took an "outsider" approach to resistance and organized ordinary people in grassroots campaigns. Other groups took an "insider" approach and worked on elections. A group that uses one approach more often than others isn't necessarily biased, but when a group has a default assumption, a home base, or a set of language choices reflecting a preference for one of the approaches, we can call that a bias in favor of that approach. Strategic biases can be positive—if we're good at one thing, it can be a superpower. The unconscious drive of our biases packs the energy, passion, and endurance that we need to move through conflict and change. What's more, a single group doesn't have to do everything; it can specialize. Groups with strategic strengths can complement each other. Recall how the organizers and the negotiators traded leading roles in fending off the replacement of Fenway Park.

A biased group can also be distracted from its goal by its allegiance to a certain approach, in the way that, if you only have a hammer, every problem looks like a nail. A group may prioritize its preferred approach over its goals; that is, it may prioritize its favorite means over its ends. Such a group will attract members who share its strategic or tactical predispositions, and it may become known for its approach more than for its goals.

Some groups put their faith in joint problem solving. They begin with the assumption that their opponents will be willing and able to negotiate a deal. Such a group has a Column A bias and will center dialogue and negotiation in their response to conflict.

Other groups perceive social relations through the lens of power differences and understand the work of conflict as a cycle of mobilizing power for incremental wins. They have a Column B bias and can be found planning protests, ginning up campaigns against more powerful forces, and cheering for the underdog.

A group with a Column C bias will lean toward resolving conflict unilaterally, because they assume that their opponents will never be able to negotiate a deal, and that deals are impossible in both the long and the short term. Their methods may vary, but their approach will be to beat the people, the forces, the institutions, or the systems that stand in the way of their goal.

As individuals, we may be biased toward talking or toward confrontation, depending on our family culture, our socioeconomic class, and our cultural customs. We may feel more or less comfort with authorities, and we may be more or less eager to take risks. Influenced by the cognitive biases of its constituents, a group may develop a tendency to approach conflict and change by problem solving (Column A), power building (Column B), or vanquishing (Column C). A group whose constituents share an inclination to fear confrontation will likely wind up with a Column A bias when facing new conflict, and a group whose constituents share the identity of social outsiders may well wind up with a bias toward Column B or Column C.

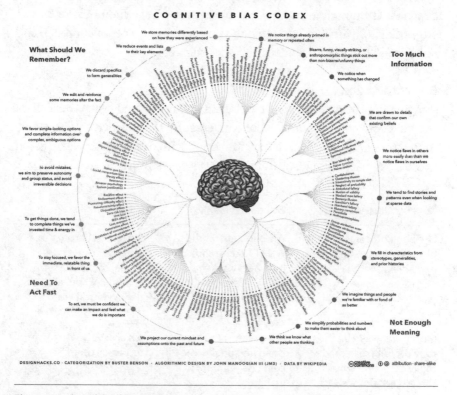

Figure 8.1: Cognitive bias codex
Created by Buster Benson and John Manoogian III, designhacks.co; reprinted with permission.

A group may be influenced as much by its context as by the biases of its constituents. It may prefer to fight, because it was formed around a fight. It may prefer confrontation as a matter of identity or of association with communities of resistance. Or it may have an articulated political theory that one approach to conflict is intrinsically better than the others.

Take a look at Figure 8.1, an illustration of hundreds of cognitive biases. From logical fallacies through evolutionary adaptations by the human brain to the way we store memories, our individual cognitive biases lead us to prefer some approaches to conflict and to avoid others. From the awareness that childhood sexual abuse forces on us to the limitations that childhood religious training places on what we permit ourselves to think to the impact of class privilege on our choices, our minds are drawn like ocean currents toward certain approaches to social interaction.

Our strategic biases fuel impulses and habits, inclinations and proclivities. Groups that know themselves and whose members acknowledge their own inclinations and habits have more choices of approach and methods. They can maximize their superpowers.

Biases in Action

Imagine you are riding a busy city bus. As you're jostled down the aisle of the bus, you overhear snippets of conversation that may give you a sense that a person or group has a bias for the specified approach. We've listed these imaginary snippets in Table 8.1. Let's eavesdrop.

Column A bias	Column B bias	Column C bias
The bank officer will probably understand if I explain patiently.	The bank officer did WHAT? There should be a law about that! Let's not waste a minute, let's get everyone to march!	Structural barriers block every avenue to real social change. That's why I believe policy reform is a waste of resources.
If only we would just take off our masks and really connect across the boundaries we've created between us.	Sure, when it affects them personally, they'll come begging for dialogue.	It's always going to be us versus them.
The one and only one way for the Israelis and Palestinians to have peace is to negotiate a deal. It may take time, but peace is worth it. There is no un-peaceful path to peace.	Resistance is the only way to justice. Our whole orientation needs to be resist, resist, resist.	The only way for the Israelis and Palestinians to have peace is for the [Israelis/Palestinians] to [keep/get] the upper hand. You can never trust the other side.

Table 8.1

Would you have been able to detect these biases?

In chapter 6, we saw how the know-and-tell cycle enables downrank people and groups to perceive the dynamics of power in ways that uprank people and groups do not. The dynamics of power allow those with less power to understand how those dynamics work, while the dynamics of power obscure themselves from those with more power. As a result, uprank groups tend to perceive social conflict as being more about the different needs, wants, cultures, hopes, and fears of different individuals and groups and less about the power dynamics among the groups in conflict. Astute uprank groups decode internal and intergroup dynamics, including the dynamics of power operating in the context of the conflict. But the nature of power makes it harder for them to see the reflections of the larger forces of structural power in their particular conflict. Unsurprisingly, this leads us to find more uprank groups with a Column A bias and more downrank groups with Column B and Column C biases.[4]

We can be biased about biases. A group that engages in dialogue doesn't necessarily have a Column A bias, any more than a group that circulates petitions or goes on strike necessarily has a Column B bias or a group that works to undermine the fossil fuel industry has a Column C bias. Imagine being at a new workplace and overhearing a group of managers talking. One says, "I suggest the teams that are fighting sit in a room and hash it out." The others agree. While this eavesdropping may lead you to think your new workplace is all about dialogue and direct communication, there may not actually be a Column A bias there. You may be witnessing good strategic thinking by principled strategists or a misplaced diagnosis of power relations, so you can't assume you are observing the workings of a group bias. Imagine that you flip on the news and hear someone announce, "We are ready to negotiate." Again, this Column A choice may be an intentional decision, not a steady habit.

Next, imagine you are privy to an email thread or Slack channel among members of a coalition working together on an issue of common concern, and you see these snippets of conversation: "If we're trying to undo racism, our staff should meet in separate caucuses for people of color and white people"; "The only way for the Israelis and Palestinians to have peace is to fight for the equal power and equal rights of Palestinians. Only then can Palestinians get a fair deal." These exchanges may or may not reflect a Column B bias. The group you're observing may be accustomed to taking different approaches under different circumstances.

Listen on the bus again, and you may hear Column C choices too: "We're going to fight the wealthy and the well-connected." "Defeating Trump was necessary but insufficient. . . . We need to mobilize to demand truly transformative solutions."[5] "The Hong Kong protesters should never agree to talks with their government. They should escalate their protests until the government steps down." "Supply and demand don't necessarily stabilize the labor market, because business controls supply, labor controls demand, and business will always have more power than labor." "Under no circumstances would I have made a deal with Hitler." Any of these statements could easily be based on an assessment of power and/or principle rather than on a Column C bias.

As you read about Column A, B, and C biases, do you find yourself insisting that you don't have a strategic bias, or are you feeling proud that you do? It's time to get real and name names. We are going to identify the mismatches groups make between strategic considerations and the approach they choose to take to conflict. And we're going to judge them. Making change is not just about what seems right. It's about what actually makes change.

Nine Biased Characters: Which One Are You?

You have seen that calculating power relations is central to choosing an effective approach to conflict. When we fail to seriously consider power relations or fail to take them into account, we can end up making choices based on less reliable factors, including our predispositions toward or against any one approach. Groups with special strengths in negotiation or in nonviolent protest or in revolution would do well to deploy those strengths in a strategically informed context. Among the nine groups we will consider, a few are aligned in this way, but most are not.

The nine fictional characters we are about to meet—tyrants, problem solvers, revolutionaries—exemplify the best and worst approaches that groups can take. These examples are based on the match, or more frequently the mismatch, between the character's relative power and their choice of approach. In Figure 8.2, we have lined up the nine characters according to three relative power scenarios: in the top row, each of the three characters is stronger than their opponents; in the middle row, they are all evenly balanced; in the bottom row, the three characters are weaker than their opponents. For each relative power scenario, we will consider three characters: one who approaches the conflict in Column A, one in Column B, and one in Column C. Nine characters altogether.

There are good guys and bad guys, confused guys and mad guys. Of course, these choices are not as simple as good and bad; power relations aren't the only arbiter of whether or not an approach is the best strategic choice. But they are ground zero for good strategy.

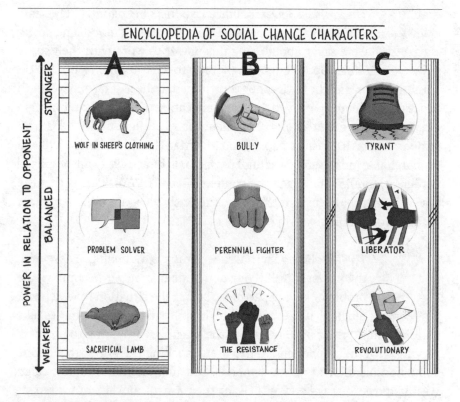

Figure 8.2: Encyclopedia of social change characters

Let's start by appraising four characters who are in the right place at the right time. They have chosen approaches that suit their power locations. We can call these four characters the conflict masters.

 The Resistance: a weaker group in Column B. When a set of people has a complaint, a demand, or a need that can be fulfilled only by someone with considerably more power, and they choose a power-building approach, they are exactly where they should be. Consider the HIV/AIDS activists in the 1980s and 1990s who fought for greater access to treatment. They plastered "silence = death" stickers on subways and toll booths, disrupted a mass at St. Patrick's Cathedral, chained themselves to the CBS evening news desk on live TV, and shut down the New York Stock Exchange. They got attention from the media and from the government agencies that they wanted to influence.

The Problem Solver: balanced partners in Column A. The same HIV/AIDS activists who were so effective at mobilizing power were savvy about using this power to work with their sometimes opponents. Their face-to-face lobbying of the US administration and the advice they contributed to the federal public health process contributed greatly to the major allocation of research funding that created the President's Emergency Plan for AIDS Relief and the Global Fund to Fight AIDS, Tuberculosis, and Malaria. The White House still had unmatchable money and structural power, but the activists had mobilized sufficient potential power in the context of the HIV/AIDS crisis that the government took them seriously. These activists recognized their moment for seizing a problem-solving approach.

The Revolutionary: a weaker group in Column C. Those with the power to fulfill our demands may never become viable problem-solving partners. This is the situation in which vanquishing is the most strategic approach. Revolutionaries take action to build their power, not for the purpose of moving to problem solving with their opponents. They aren't seeking the power to win one campaign and then make new demands. Consider the "#MeToo" campaign, with its power to take down CEOs, or the nascent movement for reparations for the descendants of enslaved Americans. Their demands will require much more than a deal or a new law; they will require an overhaul of our economic and social systems and the cultural norms that keep them in place. The revolutionary builds power to vanquish their target, whether or not that vanquishing is the ousting of an organizational leader, the overhaul of a city's criminal justice system, or the demise of the fossil fuel industry. This may involve the destruction of people or property, or it may be achieved using nonviolent methods to upend prevailing systems.

The Liberator: power symmetry in Column C. The liberator is a revolutionary with power. Liberators are positioned for violent or nonviolent battle to liberate both themselves and those on whose behalf they fight from the people or systems they seek to overthrow. Allies and accomplices of less powerful groups may be liberators, and they can do this without falling into the "savior" trap; imagine a group of white people who turn over resources and their access to resources to a movement for reparations.

These four conflict masters—the problem solver, the resistance, the revolutionary, and the liberator—do not share purposes. Problem solvers engage in joint problem solving; the resistance builds power in the present to pave the way for problem solving in the future; the revolutionary and the liberator are intent on destroying their opponents. But they share strategic clarity at the level of intentionally choosing an approach to their relationship with their opponents. We should not be surprised to find the conflict masters changing outfits as power dynamics shift, the resistance becoming the problem solver, and then possibly returning to resist some more. That's what the HIV/AIDS activists and the Fenway Park organizers did.

Each of the remaining five characters has chosen an approach that does not fit with the power dynamics in which they find themselves. We can call them dizzy disputers. Sometimes this happens because structural barriers limit a group's agency or ability to act in the conflict space. But when a group fights when it could be talking or talks when it should be fighting, awareness of the mismatch can provide an opportunity to devise an improved strategy.

Let's start in Column A.

The Wolf in Sheep's Clothing: a stronger group in Column A. As Frederick Douglass and Dr. King said, powerful groups don't give up their power without a fight. If they had sincerely intended to negotiate on equal terms, they would probably already have shared their resources and would no longer be more powerful. A powerful group in Column A may appear to be conciliatory or at least willing to negotiate a deal, but they have no genuine intention of giving up enough power to set the stage for fruitful negotiations.

There is an exception, but it is rare: the Robin Hood. A group may hold more structural and resource power than its opponents, but the more powerful group may have principled opposition to these arrangements of power. In these circumstances, where we would expect to find a wolf in sheep's clothing, we find instead a powerful individual who sincerely wishes for the power relationship to be different. Where the stronger party has a genuine commitment to the principle of a weaker party getting its needs met and its wants fulfilled, and the weaker party is aware of that commitment, both groups will, or should, choose negotiation.

It is uncommon to find a Robin Hood—and less powerful groups are right to distrust those claiming to be one—but they do exist, and groups benefit greatly from being able to identify a Robin Hood when it appears.

 The Sacrificial Lamb: a weaker group in Column A. This is the group that negotiates with the wolf. Would-be changemakers who use a problem-solving approach with their more powerful opponents produce deals that fail. A reluctance or inability to acknowledge the power asymmetry sets them up for disappointment and loss. When a stronger group sits down to negotiate with a weaker group, the more powerful group is unlikely to take the needs, concerns, and desires of the weaker group seriously. A group that finds itself in this situation needs to shift into Column B.

Let's turn our attention to Column B.

 The Perennial Fighter: power symmetry in Column B. Some organizers and activists continue to use power-building methods when they have enough power for problem solving. These are perennial fighters. They don't recognize or can't believe that they have already succeeded in acquiring the power they need to win at the negotiating table. In continuing to fight, they lose the opportunity to collect their gains. If the HIV/AIDS activists had refused invitations to speak with Centers for Disease Control officials after years of colorful but exhausting civil disobedience, they would have been perennial fighters.

We could debate the distinction between a revolutionary and a perennial fighter. When the HIV/AIDS activists met with White House officials, other HIV/AIDS activists saw them as sellouts. As campaigners on behalf of LGBTQ people, poor people, and people of color with HIV/AIDs, it was natural to self-define as perennial outsiders whose demands would never be met by the system that made them outsiders. On top of that, the activists who were negotiating had to deal with the George W. Bush administration, which was responsible for such homophobic, racist, anti-poor, and ableist policies as abstinence-only sex education and blocking federal funding for needle exchange programs. Their fellow activist critics perceived the administration the way the Libyan rebels did Gaddafi—as unworthy or incapable of joint problem solving—and, consequently, they saw themselves as revolutionaries.

The Bully: a stronger group in Column B. Like the perennial fighter, the bully uses power-building methods when they could be problem solving. But the bully doles out an extra dose of bad, because even after they have acquired more power than their opponents, and they could win what they want at the negotiating table, they instead continue ramping up their own power. For the bully, power building is no longer a means to an end; it has become the goal. Sometimes we find this type of Column B bias among social change organizers, stirred by fear or other feelings that we carry with our traumas. We may have mobilized power within social movement space, positioning ourselves to turn it against other activists as a sort of "horizontal" oppression. Organizational consultant and Black liberation movement strategist Makani Themba posted, "What does it mean when we say we are willing to die for the cause, but we are not even willing to sit down with people we don't like for the cause?"[6]

Our last character is, of course, in Column C.

The Tyrant: a stronger group in Column C. Like a bully, the tyrant exerts their power over a weaker group. The tyrant wants not only to continue building their power but to vanquish the force or system or people they perceive as blocking the way to their goals. The powerful target whom the revolutionary or liberator believes to be incapable or unworthy of joint problem solving may well be a tyrant. When the senior management team of a nonprofit organization shuts down a task force set up to address a spike in sexual harassment, they are the tyrant. So is a police force that lobs tear gas at nonviolent protesters, a justice system that concentrates its punishments on Black and Brown people, and an economic system that distributes wealth to the wealthy and crumbs to the poor. Like a bully, a tyrant uses their power against weaker people and groups. But, for the tyrant, harassing a weaker group is not enough; a tyrant seeks to neutralize, undermine, best, and destroy the power of weaker people and groups. The tyrant seeks to vanquish their weaker opponent.

A group that is aware of its strategic biases is ahead of the game in preparing for conflict. By examining the approaches we choose and the moments at which we choose them, we can grow new hope for stepping up to the heaviest challenges our communities face.

The Beauty of Awareness

My mother used to say that she truly believed in God in high school when she dissected a lobster. The colors amazed her, and the little creature's biological systems inspired her. That is how I feel around stories of groups that balance talking and fighting, strategy and principle, aspirations and the barriers around them, trauma and resilience, in a sequence that emerges from passion and planning combined.

Take, for example, a group of Black women and gender-nonconforming activists who, during the 2020 Democratic presidential campaign, knocked on doors in South Carolina—a Column B resistance activity—on behalf of Elizabeth Warren's inside-the-system Column A election campaign. They knew that one out of every three Black men born in 2001 would at some time in the future serve time behind bars,[7] and they believed that this called for structural change, a revolutionary Column C project. They were, in that sense, revolutionaries.

But consider this post from their Facebook page during the heat of the 2020 campaign:

> During a series of interviews last summer with the *New York Times*, the two most progressive candidates in this race both disappointingly & specifically named life in prison as an appropriate part of society . . . . We remain clear that [Sen. Warren] is the only candidate in this race that has an intersectional analysis on race, gender and class, is in the best position to implement structural change, and is the most willing to be accountable. We are in conversation with the campaign and are confident that this will be another example of her willingness to grow and listen.[8]

I imagine this group of activists asking themselves, "What is the strategically smart, principled path through Columns A, B, and C that will get us the best presidential candidate possible to address our moral commitments?" When they had a beef with Warren, they judged that their mobilized power had positioned them to have a productive dialogue with her campaign staff. The activists stepped into Column A with the Warren campaign, choosing to be problem solvers.[9]

Even though structural change was fundamental to this group's agenda, they did not have a Column C bias. They were conflict masters. They chose to move nimbly from revolutionary to problem solver as suited the dynamics of the situation and the associated power relationships.

I find this as stunning as my mother found that lobster.

JUST AND SOUND STRATEGY IN PRACTICE

CHAPTER 9

Rubber Meets the Road: Negotiation vs. Boycott

We're ready.

Up to this point, we've learned about the model in all its intricacies. We've seen that, when it comes to approaches to conflict, some people choose to talk and negotiate (Column A), others fight, launch protests, and undertake activities to build power (Column B), and still others set out to vanquish their opponents (Column C). There is a time for each, and groups that have mastered the process of navigating conflict will skillfully choose between the different activities and shift at appropriate moments. Those who are less self-aware may also move between the columns, but they will do so failingly, without a good strategy or a good sense of timing. These choices are influenced by four sets of factors: an understanding of power relations; structural barriers that impede strategic action; the assessment of an action against values and principles; and a group's biases and inclinations toward one approach or another.

Having covered all of this material, we're equipped to deploy the full model to help us decode a real-life example. I'm not going to choose an easy example. Instead, we're going to walk through a conflict that is long-standing and thorny. It is a story that connects intimately to my own life. And it is a conflict that is often hard to talk about: it is the tension between Israel and the Palestinians who live under Israeli governance.

In examining this conflict, I will focus on American Jews who, like me, oppose the Israeli occupation. Some oppose Israeli policies and practices in the Occupied Palestinian Territories; others have a critique of Israel that goes beyond the occupation to address the fundamental nature of an ethnically defined state. For the purposes of this analysis, we will not distinguish these critiques per se, but, rather, we will consider two divergent approaches these activists take: calling for Israeli-Palestinian negotiation and calling for a boycott of Israel. We will identify groups that have chosen different approaches to their activism. We will assess the power, structural barriers, principle, and biases each group brings, and determine which of our characters from chapter 8 can be seen at work. This story will give us the opportunity to appraise the implications of power and biases on groups' approaches to conflict in general, as well as on this particular story of struggle and change.

Ready? Let's go.

American Jews and the Occupation of Palestine

Spoiler alert: we will not solve the problem of the Israeli occupation in this chapter. But we can gain insight into it by examining the power relations in question. Israel has heavy-duty structural power, while the Palestinians live behind every type of structural barrier. Israel's parliamentary structure governs the lives of twelve million people, of whom five million are not allowed to vote. The Israel Defense Force is one of the three most powerful militaries in the world, and its gun barrels are aimed at the Palestinian half of its own population.[1] The roads in Palestine-Israel are all controlled by Israel, and most of them are off-limits to five million Palestinians. Everyone in Israel-Palestine trades in Israeli shekels, but the hundreds of army checkpoints and security barriers apply only to Palestinians.

Israel controls the resource power too. In 2018, the average per capita gross domestic product (GDP) in Israel was $41,715. The same year, per capita GDP for the West Bank and Gaza was $3,199. To put it more simply, I get thirteen apples, and you get one.[2]

Israelis travel abroad freely from a beautiful airport in Tel Aviv. But no one leaves Gaza without a good excuse and permission from Israel, which you have to secure in writing in advance. There is no operating airport in Gaza. Israel exports 10 percent of the world's cut diamonds,[3] 6.3 percent of the world's weapons parts and accessories, 5 percent of the world's armored vehicles, 4 percent of the world's pesticides, and 1.8 percent of the world's citrus products. Gaza, according to the CIA, exports "strawberries, carnations, vegetables, [and] fish (small and irregular shipments, as permitted to transit the Israeli-controlled Kerem Shalom crossing)."[4]

Israel's communications infrastructure is the most highly developed in the Middle East. The CIA reports that 100 percent of the Israeli population has access to 3G, 4G, and now 5G cell service.[5] Meanwhile, in the West Bank, Israel authorizes the allocation of frequencies and, until 2018, banned 3G service.[6] In Gaza, Israel has still not permitted access beyond 2G cell service.[7]

Who perceives this inequality most keenly? Those who experience it—Palestinians living under Israeli occupation. There are multiple levels of tyranny: Gaza residents are the poorest, most locked-in, and most vulnerable to Israeli air power. Thirty miles away, Palestinians on the West Bank experience the setup most akin to South African apartheid. They live in communities disconnected from one another by the threat of imprisonment or death, threats enforced by soldiers whose duty is to protect the Jewish settler communities built among Palestinian villages. The Palestinians in the rest of the land that we call Israel live and work as marginalized citizens in a country that celebrates Jewish culture, while demonizing Arab culture. Israel can punish Palestinians for holding an activity honoring Naqba Day, a day of mourning commemorating the mass displacement of Palestinians that accompanied Israel's founding. Aspiration for a multireligious, multiethnic democratic state is moot; according to Israel's 2018 nation-state law, "The exercise of the right to national self-determination in the State of Israel is unique to the Jewish people."[8]

Some people call Israel an apartheid state, while others consider that term abhorrent. However you describe the situation, the Gaza and West Bank Palestinian experience and the Israeli Jewish experience of politics, economics, freedom of movement, and personal safety are separate and unequal. People everywhere with a mindset oriented toward fairness perceive Israeli-Palestinian inequality, and the movement for Palestinian liberation from inequality, oppression, and occupation has gained momentum over the past decades.

American Jews are split. As Jonathan Weisman wrote in the *New York Times* in 2019, "Older American Jews, more viscerally aware of the Holocaust and connected to the living history of the Jewish state, are generally willing to look past Israeli government actions that challenge their values. Or they embrace those actions. Younger American Jews do not typically remember Israel as the David against regional Goliaths. They see a bully, armed and indifferent."[9]

The Israeli occupation of Palestine can be a very hard topic of conversation among Jews who disagree. A lot of us avoid it, because the disagreements sound like this:

Jewish Person #1: You're a tormentor. Or at least you support tormentors. That makes you a tormentor. And an oppressor.

Jewish Person #2: Me an oppressor! You are the oppressor. You oppress your own people. You, you are responsible for the murder of your own people.

Jewish Person #1: Well, you are responsible for the murder of other people. You care more about Jews than non-Jews. How can you support American democracy, such as it is, and oppose the freedom of Palestinians?

Jewish Person #2: Because the Jews are my people, and when you are persecuted worse than any people on the planet, when you survive pogroms and the Holocaust and the Arabs and Pittsburgh, you need a refuge. Where will you go if antisemitism gets worse in America? Where else but Israel?

Yet among the most active members of the anti-occupation movement in the US are American Jews. The US is Israel's biggest funder and military and political booster, and these policies are often defended in the name of American Jews. While a majority of US Jews continues to sympathize more with Israel than with Palestinians,[10] there are hundreds of thousands of Jews, possibly millions, opposed to the separate and unequal status quo. A growing number and a growing proportion of US Jews oppose Israel's occupation of Palestinian people and land.[11]

It is these anti-occupation Jews whom we will study in this chapter. Among US Jews who oppose the Israeli occupation, some take action in Column A and some in Column B, while others choose a Column C approach. To maximize the value of this exercise, we will focus on two of the approaches advocated over the past two decades by American anti-occupation Jews: negotiation and boycott.

What makes some Jewish-American opponents of the Israeli occupation choose the Column A negotiation strategy and others prefer the Column B boycott strategy?

Negotiation

Since 1991, half a dozen official deals have been signed between Israel and the Palestine Liberation Organization, all attempting to address the interests and concerns of Israel and the Palestinians.[12] Many US Jews opposed to the occupation focus their efforts on advocating for negotiations like these in the hope that they will lead to a durable agreement. Americans for Peace Now, a Jewish advocacy group, calls for "a viable, conflict-ending peace agreement between Israel and its Palestinian neighbors."[13] J Street, an American Jewish group founded in 2007, whose members identify as "pro-Israel, pro-peace," wants "a political agreement that will finally resolve the core issues driving the Israeli-Palestinian conflict."[14] These and other groups backing this approach have also tended to support a strong US role in efforts to broker a deal.

It is readily apparent that this call for negotiation is a Column A approach. The very definition of Column A delineates the method used as joint and consensual. "Joint" means that the opponents are both, or all, involved in this activity. Regardless of how happy they are to be there, how much they interrupt each other, or the tone of the dialogue, participants in negotiation engage according to a shared set of expectations. "Consensual" means that all who participate in negotiation agreed to be there, however reluctantly. In calling for negotiation, these groups have taken a Column A approach. Negotiations are a joint consensual activity, the quintessential Column A method. Negotiations may not be amicable, but their participants enter of their own volition.

How do those who back negotiations understand the power balance between Israel and the Palestinians? Let's consider the possible interpretations of their choice to act in Column A.

We might think that those who back negotiation perceive the Palestinians' power as roughly even with Israel's, since Column A activity between opponents is warranted by power symmetry. They certainly don't believe that the Palestinians have more power than Israel; if they did, they wouldn't perceive the occupation as a problem. Yet many in the pro-negotiation camp view Israel as under siege from angry Palestinians and hostile countries in the region and do not perceive Israel as significantly more powerful than the Palestinians. Perhaps they think that Israel's military strength puts Israel on equal, rather than more powerful, footing with the Palestinians. Or they may believe that Israel is indeed more powerful but genuinely wishes for the relations of power to shift. According to this belief, Israel would be the Robin Hood character we described in chapter 8.

Alternatively, these groups of American Jews may perceive Israel as stronger but may back Israel's stronger position because of a belief that this superior strength is necessary to prevail over the Palestinians to maintain Israel's own security. If this is the case, the American negotiation backers apparently believe that negotiation is a better approach regardless of the power relations between Israel and the Palestinians. When that is true, we can infer that factors other than power relations have a greater influence on their approach to the occupation. Affirming this inference, Americans for Peace Now (APN) and J Street don't tend to frame their strategies in terms of the relative power of Israelis and Palestinians. A search of APN's website turns up six references to the word "power" between 2013 and 2019, and one of these is in a piece about former US Ambassador Samantha Power.

Those who back negotiation put the Palestinians in the position of the sacrificial lamb, subject to the Israeli wolf in sheep's clothing. This dynamic can be expected to result in a downrank group settling for less than they need or want. Any deal it produces would be weak. Indeed, despite decades of successive negotiations and agreements, none has been sufficient to grant Palestinians their rights or resolve the struggle.

What might influence the thinking of this set of American Jews more than a consideration of the relationships of power? It could be a question of principle. Standing up to the traditionally pro-Israel mainstream of the American Jewish community is divisive, and the idea that some American Jews might prefer a nonconsensual or confrontational approach to Israel likely feels to many like a betrayal of familial and community loyalty. Those who are committed to the principles of loyalty and community cohesion will favor negotiation. While others might regard adhesion to the principles of loyalty and community cohesion as biases, these groups feel differently. For them, loyalty and community cohesion are not only higher priorities than strategy—they are higher priorities than resolving the needs and addressing the concerns, hopes, and fears of the Palestinians.

Of course, those who prefer negotiation are not the only ones affected by principles and biases. These are equally in play among American Jewish activists operating in Column B.

Boycott

The organized boycott of Israel and Israeli goods is a response to a call for boycott, divestment, and sanctions (BDS) put forth by Palestinians in 2005. The "Palestinian Civil Society Call for BDS" was issued by a coalition of 163 Palestinian civic and political groups, including organizations within Palestine-Israel and others in the Palestinian diaspora. Proponents of the boycott, which is meant to echo the global boycott of apartheid South

Africa in the 1980s, aim to pressure Israel to take three actions: end the occupation of the West Bank and East Jerusalem and the effective colonization of Gaza, recognize equal rights for Palestinian citizens of Israel, and protect the rights of Palestinian refugees to return to their homes in Israel.[15]

Jewish Voice for Peace (JVP) is the most prominent group of Jewish BDS backers in the United States. JVP members, like the negotiation backers, call on supporters to "help us end the occupation in our lifetimes," but theirs is not a Column A approach. Instead, JVP wants American Jews to "stand shoulder to shoulder with Palestinians in their nonviolent struggle for freedom, justice, and equality."[16] JVP engages in boycott and other forms of nonviolent struggle in solidarity with Palestinians and against the Israeli government. As such, it uses a Column B method, a unilateral and nonconsensual approach to the occupation. The classic Column B goal is to bolster the strength of the Palestinians to the point where Israel and the Palestinians could negotiate as equals.

Regardless of the details of their critique, critics of the Israeli occupation consistently note that Israel has more military and political power than the Palestinians. That is inherent in the definition of occupation. Only principle or bias could prevent a critic of the occupation from recognizing this power imbalance. As we saw above, some critics of the occupation who recognize the power imbalance may still stay in Column A, because, for reasons of loyalty and community cohesion, they find it impossible to act strategically. Again, once you understand that Column A requires power balance, only principle or bias would keep you in Column A in the case of Israel-Palestine.

Here is where this situation can get very difficult—at least for me and many others who share my cultural heritage. In chapter 8, the model characterized any group that uses power over a weaker opponent as either a bully or a tyrant. Yet from childhood, I sang, celebrated, and embraced a love for the story and feeling we called Israel. I learned about Israel and committed to it as a religious prophecy that was coming to pass in my lifetime. Inside this story, Israel isn't a bully or a tyrant—it isn't even a country; it is my homeland. It isn't a state; it is a promise of security for my people. Ben Gurion Airport isn't a transportation hub; it is a landing place for my spirit. The land isn't only a fertile crescent; it is history, it is family, and it is wonder. I am a self-loving American Jew, the child of American Jews, grandchild of Jewish immigrants who fled inhospitable conditions in late nineteenth-century Eastern Europe. The idea of Israel as bully, let alone tyrant, seems more than wrong, more than impossible. It is terrifying. It denies homeland, faith, security, history, family, and wonder.

Not only am I personally conflicted, but I know that as soon as I apply the model to Israel I will lose some of you. You will think that my whole thesis must be wrong; the proof of this lies in the impossibility that our beloved homeland, the land containing Jerusalem, the Jerusalem containing my great-grandparents' graves on the Mount of Olives, could be anything but good. The city that holds my Uncle Abe's house, built in 1939, with the name Subar inscribed on the cornerstone, our place of pilgrimage, as my brother calls it, is good. The house at 20 Malachi where, in 1968, the cab from the airport dropped my father off on his first pilgrimage, is a good house. At this house, in 1977, the cab from the airport dropped me off for my year of study in Jerusalem. From this house, I left for the West Bank Settlement of Ofra to build Jewish community on reclaimed land. We were, we are, we always will be the ones with the claim to this land that I studied to prepare for pop quizzes at Hillel School. We are not murderers. Our country is not a land of tyrants. The murderer who rises before dawn to kill the poor and needy, who comes like a thief in the night—that is the tyrant.[17] If such a thief, caught in the act of breaking in, is beaten to death, it is not even murder.[18] This is our home, not their home. We are good, and we would not steal anything, let alone someone's house. That is how we know we did not steal the land. We should be good to the stranger among us. This is not optional; we were strangers in the land of Egypt, and just as we have championed the freedom to wear a kippah to public schools in America, we must be good to the stranger among us in our homeland.[19] But let there be no misreading: he is a stranger.

In *Teaching to Transgress*, bell hooks wrote about her childhood doubts and budding critiques of the patriarchal construct her African American family enforced on itself. Although this construct was a response to systemic racism, hooks saw it as an extension of oppression rather than an antidote. The family did not welcome young hooks's challenges. Their response made her think with envy of Dorothy in *The Wizard of Oz* and wish "that she could travel to her worst fears and nightmares only to find at the end that 'there is no place like home.'" Instead, hooks found her liberation in creating theory, in "making sense out of what was happening." Of this process, she writes: "I found a place where I could imagine possible futures, a place where life could be lived differently. This 'lived' experience of critical thinking, of reflection and analysis, became a place where I worked at explaining the hurt and making it go away." Theory, she found, could be a healing place.[20]

I also find that theory can be a healing place—though a lonely one. My direct gaze back into what was happening around me in childhood and young adulthood evokes a sense of the roughness of a rusty saw. I find that criticizing Israel elicits in many a response that feels, to me, like hell. Going further and supporting a Column B approach to ending the occupation gets an even worse response. I realize that healing from my community of origin requires distance from it. For me, the price of homeland is steep.

I do not like these truths, but they are self-evident: that the Israeli state has either accepted the use of power against less powerful people or perceives the Palestinians as more powerful than itself.

If a person is reluctant to call Israel a tyrant, they will be reluctant to see Israel as the more powerful party going after the weaker one and seeking to keep it weak, because that is the work of the tyrant. This reluctance to call Israel a tyrant could surely lead a person to see the Palestinians as more powerful. Can it be true that the Palestinians are more powerful?

Palestinians do not hold structural power, but they have mobilized their potential power as the resistance and the revolution, in Column B and Column C. Over the decades, Palestinians have held weekly marches against the separation barrier that Israel erected to divide Palestinians from Jewish settlements. They rose up in the first and the second intifadas, sometimes with general strikes and sometimes with suicide bombings. Israel flew helicopter gunships over Gaza. Some Palestinians sent rockets over the boundary into Israel. Israel killed 2,139 Palestinians in the 2014 Gaza War, and Palestinians killed 64 Israelis.[21] For months, Gazans faced Israeli tear gas and bullets as they protested at the border barrier every Friday. Some of their children responded to Israeli military incursions by throwing stones. Earlier, Palestinians on the West Bank and Gaza founded the BDS movement. Acting in Column C, some Palestinians have bombed busses, hijacked planes, and murdered athletes in Munich. While Palestinian readers might dispute which of their acts of resistance were in Column B and which in Column C, all of these actions were intended either to equalize power or to vanquish Israel or Israelis.

As surely as my Jewish antecedents at Masada and my distant cousins in the Warsaw Ghetto and Birkenau prided themselves on their slingshots against the Goliaths they confronted, Palestinian resistance fighters have sought to bolster their causes with tactical wins. As bravely as European Jewish refugees laid claim to Palestinian land in the 1930s by smuggling concrete blocks to hilltops in the night and at daybreak presenting the faits accomplis of legal Jewish villages by virtue of having one wall and a speedily erected tower, Palestinian resistance fighters have strategized, lost, won, won, and lost. Slingshots are neither inherently right nor inherently good, just as we might say about negotiations. But they can be steps toward negotiation, if not liberation. But but but but but. . .

From the Associated Press, in 2016:

> The Israeli government recently allotted nearly $26 million in this year's budget to combat what it sees as worldwide efforts to "delegitimize" the Jewish state's right to exist. Some of the funds are earmarked for Israeli tech companies, many of them headed by former military intelligence officers, for digital initiatives aimed at gathering intelligence on activist groups and countering their efforts.[22]

The boycott of Israel is seen by many Jews as delegitimizing Israel, and, to many, this means delegitimizing Jews. This chain of association, combined with the need that many Jews feel for loyalty and belonging to the Jewish community, especially in the face of real antisemitism, has biased many American Jews against the boycott and against BDS more generally. We don't want to be vulnerable to harm from our communities or from outsiders.

The majority of American Jews, including my family, even those who oppose the occupation, cannot accept that it is natural, inevitable, good, and right for Palestinians and humanitarians to use principled Column B activity to shift power.

Do you hear my reluctance? I am giving voice to a reluctance I have genuinely felt over the course of my lifetime, but I am not, in the moment of writing this, actually reluctant. This story is my way of arming my memory against the hurt of Kansas and the alienation of Oz, as I still seek healing in the promised land of true stories, hardheaded theory, and the principles of justice and love.

In a January 2019 column in the *New York Times*, author Michelle Alexander described the forces at work that inhibit concerned Americans from speaking out fully for Palestinian freedom. She named "the excuses and rationalizations that have kept me largely silent on one of the great moral challenges of our time: the crisis in Israel-Palestine." The pressure is not subtle for either Jewish or non-Jewish progressives. As Alexander explained:

> Many civil rights activists and organizations have remained silent as well, not because they lack concern or sympathy for the Palestinian people, but because they fear loss of funding from foundations, and false charges of anti-Semitism. They worry, as I once did, that their important social justice work will be compromised or discredited by smear campaigns. . .
>
> Just as Dr. King received fierce, overwhelming criticism for his speech condemning the Vietnam War—168 major newspapers, including The Times, denounced the address the following day—those who speak publicly in support of the liberation of the Palestinian people still risk condemnation and backlash. . .[23]
>
> [King] said, "A time comes when silence is betrayal" and added, "that time has come for us in relation to Vietnam."
>
> It was a lonely, moral stance. And it cost him. But it set an example of what is required of us if we are to honor our deepest values in times of crisis, even when silence would better serve our personal interests or the communities and causes we hold most dear.[24]

My healing comes through making sense of the world around me. Israel is in Column C, acting to vanquish the power of Palestinians. It is, by my definition, a tyrant. The boycotters are building power to weaken Israel's negotiating position so that, as Palestinians gain power, Israel will be compelled, nonviolently forced, to come to the table. The boycotters are in Column B, building power to pave the way for Palestinians to arrive at Column A, together with Israel, once power is equalized. Only when that happens can we credibly hope for a durable negotiated arrangement that will succeed in addressing all Israeli and Palestinian needs, desires, fears, and hopes.

Biases

When we talked about structural barriers, we gave a name to the phenomenon of uprank groups failing to perceive the power dynamics that downrank groups experience and understand: "know-and-tell." Downrank groups perceive the workings of power more acutely than do uprank groups. Where downrank groups have the benefit of this perception of power relations, uprank groups have an inherent bias against perceiving the big picture of power relations. As a result, an uprank group doesn't necessarily know that it is an uprank group. Even were members of an uprank group aware that uprank groups are biased against perceiving the prevailing power relations, they would not necessarily recognize their own privileged position.

The know-and-tell dynamic is structural; it's like physics. It doesn't discriminate between senior management teams, bank executives, white people, and cisgender straight men. Uprank groups, by definition, write the rules of the game, and those whom the rules don't suit become, by definition, the downrank groups. Anti-occupation American Jews tend to be progressives within the US political context. As progressives, and even as Jews, they may know that attention follows power and that uprank groups don't perceive their own power. But those who believe that Israel and the Palestinians should negotiate a settlement before equalizing power are biased by the know-and-tell phenomenon against accurately analyzing the Israeli-Palestinian power dynamic.

Chapter 6 introduced know-and-tell in the context of barriers, and now we can see its relationship to biases. Because powerful people naturally misperceive, they need to take initiative if they are to correctly understand the realities of the lives of people with less power. Without extra work, they will not be able to perceive these realities accurately, however good their intentions may be. Thus, men must work actively to perceive the reality of women's lives if they are to understand the dynamics of patriarchy. Christians must make an effort to grasp the realities of Jewish lives, and of both overt and subtle antisemitism. Similarly, Jews must work to recognize the fundamental humanity of Muslims and reckon with Islamophobia. Straight people have to work to understand how heteronormativity affects lesbian, gay, and queer people, and cisgender people have to work to perceive the range of trans experience. I and my fellow white people need to make an effort if we are to recognize that our society treats Black people as if their lives do not matter and act on that knowledge.

This lack of perception applies specifically to the powerful. It is very easy for the weak to perceive that the lives of the powerful matter more to society than do their own lives. So while the work of the powerful is to grasp that the other matters and to learn how that basic fact is ignored at great peril, the work of the weak is to recognize that they themselves matter.

That I am aware of some of my biases and unaware of others is an article of faith. It does not prevent me from perceiving others' biases, but it makes me unreliable in perceiving dynamics downrank from me. While each of us knows something about our own biases, none of us knows everything about our own biases. The more we pay attention to those downrank from us and question what we perceive, the more carefully we sense the dynamics of the relationships among us, and the more we question, the more our choices will be rational. Paying attention and acting rationally based on reality becomes a moral duty.

When I was eighteen and spent a week in the West Bank settlement of Ofra, I lived with a group of religious Jewish women my age who were skipping army service to volunteer in newly settled Jewish communities. The women slept in trailers, and and a group of young men volunteers stayed in a building called Beit Ha-Sheikh. You could pronounce the name of that building as if it was a single word, but if you stopped to listen to yourself, you realized that at some point in history that long stone house just inside Ofra's barbed-wire gate was the grand residence of the local sheikh, the head of the local Muslim community.

On Saturday night at Ofra, the other young women and I got a dusty ride down to the gate in a pickup, stopped to pick up our friends at Beit Ha-Sheikh, and continued on to Jerusalem to flirt with boys at a candlelit café called Chocolate Soup. It was magical, and the memory remained magical, until I started trying to account for the missing sheikh and his missing community. Where did they go?

Seventy-six percent of American Jews say they are emotionally attached to Israel.[25] It should not be surprising that they are biased toward believing that our own people cannot be tyrants. I don't begrudge my people our safety. I don't even mind us having a land to call home, although universalism is as close to home as my queer self can come. I believe Jews should have free access to pray in our old synagogues and at our gravesites. I think it is good to have public celebrations of Jewish holidays and living Jewish languages, Hebrew and also Yiddish, Arabic, and the other languages of the Jewish diaspora. But this cannot be right unless the same is true for Palestinians. Practicing Muslims and Christians must be equally free to pray at their holy sites. Arabic must be no less an official language than Hebrew. The security system must equally protect all twelve million people on the land, and they must all be entitled to citizenship on the same terms. They must all have an equal say in the government that manages their affairs. If there is to be a flag, it must equally and visibly stand for all its people.

The individuals in both the negotiation and the boycott camps have biases toward membership in their own groups. We all want to belong, so we hesitate to betray the party line. Our decisions are all influenced by desires for loyalty, justice, fairness, truth, and some mixture of family, Jewish tradition, Jewish survival, and respect for the lives of others. We rank these concerns differently, however. Generally speaking, the Column A negotiation proponents prioritize loyalty and Jewish community cohesion, and the Column B supporters prioritize universality and justice.

Safe Home

The desire for a safe home is natural. My grandmother taught me not to raise my voice, to wear gloves to shul, and to sit like a lady. We talked our way, gently and rationally, through difficulties. I didn't do any of these things well, but I still often gravitate toward the aesthetics of politeness, civility, and reasonable tones of voice. I was raised to talk, and certainly not to fight. I experienced this as the bias of a second-generation middle-class family aspiring to belong in America. Yes, I have a bias toward universalism, but I also have this strong Column A bias that comes from the specific ways in which my family tried to create a safe home in the United States.

This same desire for a safe home has led Israel to pursue the occupation of Palestinian people. Thinking of Israel as their people's safe home has prevented some American Jews from seeing the power of Israel's military violence and state-sponsored racism for the tyranny that they are. My conclusion is not that Israel is worse than anyone else but the very opposite—that Israel is ordinary. That the leadership of Jews does not magically make a country a light to the nations. That being Jewish-led does not make an army moral. That Israel is a country, not a god. The fact that it hurts to unpack these myths does not make it acceptable to preserve them. The fact that a group holds Column B strategies to be disloyal or otherwise distasteful does not mean that they can achieve their goals in Column A.

The strategic, principled, rational, and compassionate approach for American Jews would be to make sure that the desire for a safe and peaceful home for some does not obscure the need for a safe and peaceful home for all. Gazan farmers get to harvest and sell their crops in season and to exchange their profits for farm machines, seeds, and groceries for their families, not because they are Palestinian or because they are good people, any more than Jews deserve groceries for being moral, but because we are all human. The humane approach requires a principled strategy for changing the power dynamics between the Palestinians and Israel. Until the power is equal, we cannot expect negotiation to prevail.

CHAPTER 10

Conclusion

> Reach down, punch up.
> —Kati Sipp, organizer

I have spent most of sixty years trying to make sense of a world that never fits my body or my sensibilities, a world filled with square pegs and round holes, food everywhere and hungry people by the billions. The global pandemic of 2020 has appeared, and now the world makes no sense to anyone, and I feel, in an odd way, better. I can maneuver with ease when nobody knows if the sun will come up tomorrow. I may die, but I get it: nothing is in order, and the bottom that dropped out when I left my community at age twenty-five has now dropped out for everyone.

But as the plague tightens I do too, bunching up my long bones and tightening my thighs, trying not to lose control. This is my spot on the bench. I have to hold tight to my spot, because safety is scarce. This is not new; when women have struggled, for example, we have all been on the side of the women. But the dynamics of the scarcity of safety have been freshly laid bare. Unless we ourselves or our ancestors were enslaved, we thought we had freed the slaves, but we never did free the slaves. We never did create safety for Jews or immigrants or Kalmyks or queers. People with twisted bodies and dysfunctional emotional lives have never been safe. Now the secret is out, which always feels better: we are all in trouble together.

When to Fight

> and when we speak we are afraid
> our words will not be heard
> nor welcomed
> but when we are silent
> we are still afraid
>
> So it is better to speak
> Remembering
> we were never meant to survive.
> —Audre Lorde[1]

The older kids will get the food. The stronger kids will get picked for the team. The pretty ones will get the dates. Only the brains of the lightest-skinned ones will be noticed. The quick-witted and easygoing will be fine. The Christians will be normal. The homeowners will be cared for. The rich will be first in line. The cool kids will win.

We don't want to be thrown out of the garden or voted off the island. We want to live, and that is frightening. Change is terrifying. Who will protect us? If we are worried that we are beholden to others for our food or for love we won't fight. We won't bite the hand that feeds us. Besides, remember what Jefferson wrote: "Mankind are more disposed to suffer, while evils are sufferable, than to right themselves by abolishing the forms to which they are accustomed."[2]

It isn't natural for us to be strategic about when to talk and when to fight. We hold back from fighting either to ensure that we are fed, or because we are not hungry enough. Either because we are afraid of freezing to death, or because we aren't the least bit bothered by the weather. In Chicago last year it was -50°F on a Thursday and +57°F by the next Monday. But it is always +72°F when you control the heat.

As a middle-class white person who has breathed the air of twentieth- and twenty-first-century America, sometimes I catch myself momentarily forgetting about inequality. I catch myself breathing and not noticing the breath going in. We do this in order to live. A dozen therapists have reminded me not to focus on road deaths when I get in the car; without some suspension of awareness, they say, you would never step foot outside.

This unconsciousness costs lives, though. We are accustomed to raising men a certain way in our cultures, and no one is *trying* to be sexist, it's true, but, at this point in history, a man's job is to unravel the damage. No one has to convince you of that. Well, if that is true about men, then as a white person, that's how powerful my motivation to undo racism needs to be.

What is the work of a white American in dismantling our American system of racism? People have worked against racial injustice since slavery, through the post–Civil War Jim Crow era, in times of legal and then illegal discrimination and judicial insults and witless subjugation at every level of our society. Then, in 2014, the news of the killings by police officers of unarmed Black men and women reached us differently. This was the Movement for Black Lives, catalyzed by the invention of social media and savvy organizers, and anti-racist voices became harder for white people to ignore. Kimberlé Crenshaw's teachings on intersectionality broke through to progressive movement spaces, into nonprofits, and into corporate human resources departments. Staff of color and allies demanded alignment between official values statements and real change.

Younger people in blue-state America have grown up into a greater culture that won't tolerate unaddressed racism. The call for more women in leadership positions is now tied to the demand for more Black and Brown people in the most senior positions. If women are to be promoted, so are trans and gender-nonconforming people and so are queer Black women. Sometimes consideration of people with disabilities is a second order thought, but the era of #BlackLivesMatter has brought a contagious vigor to organizational inclusion that encourages the widening of the circle of "we" when deficiencies are brought to light.

Most progressive organizations are led by white women, except for the bigger organizations, many of which are led by white men.[3] Their staff come to them asking: Why aren't there more people of color at this organization? Surely Black and Latinx men would be eager to work here? Why are most of the Black women here in lower-level administrative jobs and not in program positions? Why is the boss always white? Why are the rules still the rules of the ruling culture? Why is your time more important than mine? Why do you recognize the achievements of white staff so readily and not ours? Don't you hear yourselves when you put white people, white history, white needs at the center of the story?

A Black man is still fourteen times more likely to be shot to death in America than a white man.[4] Black households in America still have an average of $7,113 of wealth, if you can call it that, and Latinx households have $8,348, while the average wealth of white households is $111,146.[5] Better to block it out. It's so awful, and it makes it hard to drive, to eat, to sleep. There are too many awful things.

But the rules are still set by the powerful and enforced by our compliance. And now it is all laid bare by Black bodies and poor bodies, the bodies of hospital workers and delivery drivers, falling fast in the sieve of the pandemic. This is the occasion to be brave enough to fight.

When to Talk

Today, I passed a man walking a dog. He was Black and his beard was grey, his dog was small and black and grey, and I was not afraid of him as I walked by and nodded. It took me twenty-nine years from becoming aware of my whiteness to not being struck by a stranger's Blackness.

It is good to notice these little changes. The struggle for fairness will always be there, but that doesn't mean we never win. That doesn't mean we never rest, and it doesn't mean we always engage the fight.

When we do engage the fight against the bully or the tyrant, it doesn't mean we have to fight each other. There has to be space inside social struggle for talk among the fighters. There has to be negotiation inside protest. For a group with solid skills in Column B and Column C, the Column A practices of dialogue, negotiation, and even consensual democracy can feel like a burden. On this, activist Linda Sarsour wrote:

> Let us not fall for the longstanding tactics of white supremacy of divide and conquer...
>
> I ask you all to model how we approach each other in the movement. Have conversations, reach out, ask questions, give benefit of the doubt, contextualize moments outside of your own personal feelings, remind yourself of the good this person or persons or organization has done. Use critical thinking skills. . . . Be honest with your feelings, speak from the I, propose solutions and not demands. Challenge people in your circles, engage people. Tearing down, threatening movement leaders with "say this or else we won't do this or if you don't say this then it's meaningless" is not the way.[6]

This is possible! I went to a conference on Black Radical Traditions at Temple University in 2016. There was a question and answer period, and a Black person spoke up and said, "Maybe the white people should cede their spaces to the Black people who are waiting in the back of the room.

Maybe the white people who have yellow wrist bands because they signed up early and paid their registrations early can give their seats to those Black people." And we did!

If we recognize the humanity in each other, we can tolerate each other's inconsistencies and imperfections. We need these talking skills for the win. Change is possible. We can be brave enough to talk.

A Time You May Embrace, a Time to Refrain from Embracing[7]

We have examined the roles of power, of structural barriers, and of principle, and the role of biases toward one approach to conflict or another. We have seen that a social struggle or a conflict between management and workers may bounce back and forth among problem solving, power building, and vanquishing for years or even generations. A cast of change-seeking characters make better or worse choices about what approach to take based on an assessment of the power relations between themselves and their opponents.

Yet our choices about how we engage in conflict and social struggle don't always serve our own interests. With so much at stake in twenty-first-century America, of course, we all want to win. So many strategies and tactics, methods and tools, approaches and resources, are available to help us bring about the change we want, but many of our communities, caucuses, and committees have the habit of choosing some and avoiding others.

We encounter groups whose moral convictions commit them to the strategic nonviolence of Gandhi, the military bravery of Joan of Arc, or the calm conciliation of Mr. Rogers. Each has its time and place. Yet when it comes to conflict, we humans are particularly bad at choosing strategically. We lack confidence that our needs and desires will be fulfilled.

It is the group that has practiced strategic thinking and organized committed people in quieter times that can mobilize in moments of opportunity. Those who sharpen their tools for Column A, B, and C are prepared to face the moment that confronts us.

The tension inherent in a big, consequential decision is one we are all familiar with on a personal level. When, in January 2020, basketball star Kobe Bryant was killed in a helicopter crash with eight other victims, the usual social media tensions emerged between well-intentioned critics and fans. But activist Aly Wane felt conflicted, and he posted a beautiful description of the human experience of the talking-fighting dance:

I think Kobe Bryant meant a lot to many of us black folks, for complicated reasons.

I also believe he got away with rape.

I also think he was a great dad.

I also think he was one of the greatest players to play the game.

I also think his promotion of women's basketball and the W.N.B.A. was admirable and forward-thinking.

I also loved his aerial artistry.

I also know that sexual assault survivors will be triggered and traumatized by this public lionization.

I also know that even though I resented his seeming selfishness and political apathy in his early years, he grew into a type of maturity in his personal life and in his philanthropic endeavors that surprised me in a positive way. As he grew older, he grew bolder in his political visibility in ways that I appreciated (seeing him rock the "I can't breathe" t-shirt to commemorate Eric Garner's assassination by the police heartened me).

I also don't think that this erases the deep trauma he caused.

I also believe in healing, growth and redemption.

I also cried when I heard he died, because feelings are not political agendas and many of these celebrities are intertwined in our memories in ways that bypass our frontal cortex (I'm looking at you Michael Jackson). I remember "where I was when Kobe, the athlete, did [insert greatathleticachievement]."

I also know that the ability to compartmentalize is a luxury of the privileged, and as someone who has not been sexually abused I have privilege.

I also know that his child died with him and that she deserved a longer life.

I also mourn for his family.

I also hold his survivor and other sexual assault survivors in the light tonight.

I also know that the basketball fan in me will miss him.

This is hard to process.

Please be gentle, as best you can.

And if this reflection hurts or offends, I also believe that as an imperfect human being (like all of us), I will hurt and harm people I love.

Because such is life.
And life is very, very short.[8]

The honesty of that struggle is beautiful. Take a stand or not? Weep or struggle? Armed or not? Civil war or not? Overthrow of capitalism or not? People die or not? Prolonged or more instant change? What kind of leadership does the moment demand? Chaos and anarchy? Consensus-based decision-making? When is the time right?

Wise groups, like each of us at our wisest, play this tug of war with skill and love. For the future of our species and the health of our planet, may our communities and workplaces build change with wisely chosen strategy and practiced habits of humanity.

Notes

Foreword, Esteban Kelly

1   North American Students of Cooperation (NASCO); for more information, see www. nasco.coop.

2   Transformative justice uses instances of conflict and harm as opportunities to explore ways that communities can shift our conditions toward liberation. It is a grassroots approach to addressing systems of violence, without relying on punishment, incarceration, or policing; see Ejeris Dixon and Leah Lakshmi Piepzna-Samarasinha, eds., *Beyond Survival: Strategies and Stories from the Transformative Justice Movement* (Oakland: AK Press, 2020).

Foreword, Douglas Stone

1   Roger Fisher did not like the phrase "win-win." The goal of engaging in conflict is not to "win" but to reach a fair, durable outcome.

2   Saul Alinsky, *Rules for Radicals* (New York: Vintage, 1989 [1971]), 28.

Chapter 1: Lovers and Fighters: A Personal Story

1   John Lennon, "Imagine" (London: Apple Records, 1971).

2   Frederick Douglass, "No Progress without Struggle" (1857), Black Past, accessed December 25, 2020, https://www.blackpast.org/african-american-history/1857-frederick-douglass-if-there-no-struggle-there-no-progress.

3   "His Holiness the Dalai Lama Spends the Day on Capitol Hill," March 7, 2014, His Holiness the 14th Dalai Lama of Tibet, accessed December 25, 2020, https://tinyurl.com/y9y6psg3.

4   Howard Bryant, *The Heritage: Black Athletes, a Divided America, and the Politics of Patriotism* (Boston: Beacon Press, 2018), 6.

5   Ibid., 226.

6   Ibid., 234.

7   Ibid., 236.

8   Megan Rapinoe, "Why I Am Kneeling," Player's Tribune, October 6, 2016, accessed December 25, 2020, https://www.theplayerstribune.com/articles/megan-rapinoe-why-i-am-kneeling.

Chapter 2: To Everything a Season

1   Audre Lorde, "The Transformation of Silence into Language and Action," *The Cancer Journals* (San Francisco: Spinsters Ink, 1980).

2   Lev. 19:27.

3   Rabbi Berel Wein, "Beards," Rabbi Wein.com, accessed December 25, 2020, https://www.rabbiwein.com/blog/beards-667.html.

4   Mark Engler and Paul Engler, *This Is an Uprising: How Nonviolent Revolt Is Shaping the Twenty-First Century* (New York: Nation Books, 2016), 226.

5   "Seattle Black Panther Party History and Memory Project," Civil Rights and Labor History Project, accessed December 25, 2020, http://depts.washington.edu/civilr/BPP.htm; Kurt Schaeffer, "The Black Panther Party in Seattle, 19681970," Seattle Civil Rights and Labor History Project, accessed December 25, 2020, http://depts.washington.edu/civilr/Panthers1_schaefer.htm#_edn24.

6   Daniel Victor, "Pepsi Pulls Ad Accused of Trivializing Black Lives Matter," *New York Times*, April 5, 2017, accessed December 25, 2020, https://www.nytimes.com/2017/04/05/business/kendall-jenner-pepsi-ad.html.

7   James Rucker, "How an Advertiser Boycott Campaign Helped Push Glenn Beck off the Air," AlterNet, April 3, 2011, accessed December 25, 2020, https://tinyurl.com/ya2rujjd.

8   Van Jones, *Rebuild the Dream* (New York: Nation Books, 2012), 79.

9   Kenneth W. Thomas and Ralph H. Kilmann, "Thomas-Kilmann Conflict Mode Instrument Profile and Interpretive Report," Myers-Briggs Company, accessed December 25, 2020, https://shop.themyersbriggs.com/en/tkiproducts.aspx?pc=142.

10   Lewis Goldberg, "Language and Individual Differences: The Search for Universals in Personality Lexicons," in L. Wheeler, ed., *Review of Personality and Social Psychology*, vol. 2 (Los Angeles: Sage, 1981), 141–65.

11   David Antonioni, "Relationship between the Big Five Personality Factors and Conflict Management Styles," *International Journal of Conflict Management* 9, no. 4 (April 1998), accessed December 25, 2020, https://www.emeraldinsight.com/doi/pdfplus/10.1108/eb022814.

12   Nina Easton, "Democrats' War on Corporate Greed: Mostly Bluster," CNN Money, December 14, 2007, accessed December 25, 2020, https://tinyurl.com/y79nxefk.

13   Paul Krugman, "Opinion: Big Table Fantasies," *New York Times*, December 7, 2007, accessed December 25, 2020, https://www.nytimes.com/2007/12/17/opinion/17krugman.html.

14   Sasha Issenberg, "Edwards Brings Fighting Words," Boston.com, January 1, 2008, accessed December 25, 2020, https://tinyurl.com/yakb9vy6.

15   "Video of Heated Confrontation between American Airlines' Mechanics and Airline President Shared," CBSDFW.com, May 24, 2019, accessed December 25, 2020, https://tinyurl.com/ydxuwwuf; transcribed by the author.

16   William Zartman, *Elusive Peace: Negotiating an End to Civil Wars* (Washington, DC: Brookings Institution Press, 1995), 8.

17   From Nelson Mandela's reply to an offer of release if he renounced violence, February 10, 1985; cited in "Nelson Mandela Quotes: 'Real Leaders Must Be Ready to Sacrifice All for the Freedom of Their People,'" *Guardian*, December 6, 2013, accessed December 25, 2020, https://tinyurl.com/grkdqnu.

18   Dr. Martin Luther King, Jr., "Letter from a Birmingham Jail," April 16, 1963, African Studies Center—University of Pennsylvania, accessed December 25, 2020, https://www.africa.upenn.edu/Articles_Gen/Letter_Birmingham.html.

Chapter 3: Yes, No, or Never: When Do We Fight?

1   Frederick Douglass, "West India Emancipation," speech at Canandaigua, New York, August 3, 1857, Black Past, accessed December 25, 2020, https://tinyurl.com/ycybds6h.
2   Gene Sharp, *Politics of Nonviolent Action, Part Two: The Methods of Nonviolent Action* (Boston: Porter Sargent Books, 2000).
3   Dan Berger, *Outlaws of America: The Weather Underground and the Politics of Solidarity* (Oakland: AK Press, 2006), 162.
4   Lacey, who is gender nonbinary, uses the pronoun "they"; for more on use of the singular pronoun "they," see singularthey.info.
5   Dr. Martin Luther King, Jr., "Letter from a Birmingham Jail," April 16, 1963, African Studies Center—University of Pennsylvania, accessed December 25, 2020, https://www.africa.upenn.edu/Articles_Gen/Letter_Birmingham.html.
6   See, for example, Kwame Ture (formerly known as Stokely Carmichael) and Charles V. Hamilton, *Black Power: The Politics of Liberation in America* (Toronto: Random House, 1967).
7   "Statement of Alabama Clergymen" (letter to Dr. Martin Luther King, Jr.), April 12, 1963, The Estate of Martin Luther King, Jr., accessed December 25, 2020, https://tinyurl.com/y7d54kks.
8   King, "Letter from a Birmingham Jail."
9   "Rebels Will Not Negotiate with Gaddafi" (video), RT America, August 29, 2011, accessed December 25, 2020, https://www.youtube.com/watch?v=C9oL7zhFUqw; United Nations Security Council Resolution 1973, March 17, 2011, accessed December 25, 2020, http://www.un.org/ga/search/view_doc.asp?symbol=S/RES/1973%20%282011%29.

Section II Factors in Choosing to Talk or Fight

1   Ella Baker, as quoted by Marian Wright Edelman, "Ella Baker: My Civil Rights Generation's 'Fundi'," March 28, 2014, accessed December 25, 2020, https://tinyurl.com/ycf7e4t7.

Chapter 4: Power

1   Definitions can be attributed respectively to Starhawk: "the power that emerges from within, that is inherent in us as the power to grow is inherent in seed"; Starhawk, *Truth or Dare: Encounters with Power, Authority, and Mystery* (San Francisco: Harper, 1987), 8; Jean Baker Miller: "the capacity to produce a change—that is, to move anything from point A or state A to point B or state B"; Jean Baker Miller, "Women and Power," in Thomas Wartenberg, ed., *Rethinking Power* (Albany, NY: SUNY Press, 1992), 241; Bertrand Russell: "the production of intended effects"; Bertrand Russell, *Power: A New Social Analysis* (London: Unwin Books, 1975 [1938]), 35; Hannah Arendt: "the human ability not just to act but to act in concert"; Hannah Arendt, *On Violence* (New York: Harcourt Harvest Book, 1970), 44; Max Weber: "the probability that one actor within a social relationship will be in a position to carry out his own will despite resistance regardless of the basis on which this probability

rests"; Max Weber, Guenther Roth, and Claus Wittich, *Economy and Society: An Outline of Interpretive Sociology* (Berkeley: University of California Press, 1978 [1922]), 53; Robert Dahl: "*A* has power over *B* to the extent that he can get *B* to do something that *B* would not otherwise do"; Robert Dahl, "The Concept of Power," *Behavioral Science* 2, no. 3 (1957): 202–3, accessed December 25, 2020, http://fbaum. unc.edu/teaching/articles/Dahl_Power_1957.pdf.

2   Roger Fisher, William Ury, and Bruce Patton, *Getting to Yes*, 2nd ed. (New York: Penguin, 1991), 97–106.

3   For the history of the Philadelphia Public Access Corporation, or PhillyCAM, see PhillyCAM, *Philadelphia Community Media Access Strategic Plan FY 2013 through FY 2018* (Philadelphia: PhillyCAM, 2012), 16, accessed December 25, 2020, https:// phillycam.org/sites/default/files/StrategicPlan_Final_6_27_12.pdf.

Chapter 5: Currencies of Power

1   For an overview of definitions of power, see introduction to Steven Lukes, ed., *Power* (New York: New York University Press, 1986).

2   Michel Foucault, *The History of Sexuality, Volume 1: An Introduction*, trans. Robert Hurley (New York: Vintage, 1979), 92–93.

3   Alexandria Ocasio-Cortez (@AOC), Twitter, March 21, 2019, 4:26 p.m., accessed December 25, 2020, https://twitter.com/aoc/status/1108827309082062848?lang =en.

4   Martin Luther King, Jr., "Beyond Vietnam" (audio), Riverside Church, New York City, April 4, 1967, Stanford: Martin Luther King, Jr. Research and Education Institute, accessed December 25, 2020, https://kinginstitute.stanford.edu/king-papers/ documents/beyond-vietnam.

5   Ibid.

6   Thomas Jefferson et al., "Declaration of Independence" (Philadelphia, 1776), National Archives, accessed December 25, 2020, https://www.archives.gov/founding-docs/ declaration-transcript.

7   In Tunisia, as in many post-revolutionary states, many liberatory aspirations that came to pass did not endure.

8   Ashley Southall, "'Appalling' Video Shows the Police Yanking 1-Year-Old from His Mother's Arms," *New York Times*, December 9, 2018, accessed December 25, 2020, https://tinyurl.com/yazfoaxe; Nikita Stewart, "$625,000 Settlement for Woman Whose Child Was Torn From Her Arms," *New York Times*, December 13, 2019, accessed December 25, 2020, https://tinyurl.com/ybxgmyw6; "SMH" is a social media abbreviation for "shaking my head."

9   See Thomas C. Shelling, *Arms and Influence* (New Haven: Yale University Press, 1966), especially Chapter 1, "The Diplomacy of Violence."

10   For more on mobilizing power, see Marshall Ganz, "Organizing: People, Power, and Change; Organizing Notes, Charts, Reflection Questions," accessed December 25, 2020, https://tinyurl.com/ycdm4qsf.

11   Pema Levy, "Facebook Just Released Its New Plan for Protecting Your Civil Rights," *Mother Jones*, June 30, 2019, accessed December 25, 2020, https://tinyurl.com/ yd3fjeg8.

12   See Gene Sharp, *Politics of Nonviolent Action, Part Two: The Methods of Nonviolent Action* (Boston: Porter Sargent Books, 2000).

13 James Baldwin, *The Fire Next Time* (New York: Vintage International, 1993 [1963]), 48–49.

14 See Jo Freeman aka Joreen, "The Tyranny of Structureless," Jo Freeman.com, accessed December 25, 2020, http://www.jofreeman.com/joreen/tyranny.htm; website version based on 1970, 1971, and 1972 publications.

Chapter 6: Structural Barriers

1 "Iraqi Peace Activist Forced to Change T-Shirt Bearing Arabic Script Before Boarding Plane at JFK" (transcript), *Democracy Now*, August 21, 2006, accessed December 25, 2020, https://www.democracynow.org/2006/8/21/iraqi_peace_activist_forced_to_change.

2 Thucydides, "The Melian Dialogue," book 5, chap. 17 (c. 431), in *The History of the Peloponnesian Wars*, trans. Richard Crawley, accessed December 25, 2020, https://history.hanover.edu/courses/excerpts/211thuc.html.

3 Susan T. Fiske, "Controlling Other People: The Impact of Power on Stereotyping," in Nancy Rule Goldberger and Jody Bennet Veroff, eds. *The Culture and Psychology Reader* (New York: New York University Press, 1995), 444.

4 Ibid.

5 W. E. B. Du Bois, "The Souls of Black Folk," in *Three Negro Classics* (New York: Avon Books, 1965 [1910]), 214–15.

6 "Status and Trends in the Education of Racial and Ethnic Groups," National Center for Education Statistics, updated February 2019, accessed December 25, 2020, https://nces.ed.gov/programs/raceindicators/indicator_RDC.asp; John Gramlich, "The Gap Between the Number of Blacks and Whites in Prison Is Shrinking," Pew Research Center, April 30, 2019, accessed December 25, 2020, https://tinyurl.com/y9otr4ez; Tylor Telford, "Income Inequality in America Is the Highest It's Been Since Census Bureau Started Tracking It, Data Show," *Washington Post*, September 26, 2019, accessed December 25, 2020, https://tinyurl.com/y5ugcdsd.

7 "Vision for Black Lives," M4BL, accessed December 25, 2020, https://m4bl.org/policy-platforms.

8 Cassandra Monique Batie (aka Andra Day) and Jennifer Decilveo, "Rise Up" (video with lyrics), YouTube, accessed December 25, 2020, https://www.youtube.com/watch?v=FBuIBaDSOa4.

9 Charles P. Pierce, "Parchman State Prison Is Like the Vestibule of Hell," *Esquire*, January 9, 2020, accessed December 25, 2020, https://tinyurl.com/ycn6m65e.

10 John Bowden, "Border Patrol Denies Claims of Orders to Detain Iranian Americans," *Hill*, January 5, 2020, accessed December 25, 2020, https://tinyurl.com/yaqtyovv.

11 James Baldwin, *The Fire Next Time* (New York: Vintage International, 1993 [1963]), 103.

12 William Wordsworth, "Ode: Intimations of Immortality from Recollections of Early Childhood" (1804), Poetry Foundation, accessed December 25, 2020, https://tinyurl.com/y349klj4.

13 Du Bois, "The Souls of Black Folk," 214; in the original publication of the first chapter of *Souls of Black Folks* in the *Atlantic*, the words "shades of the prison-house" appear in quotation marks; see W. E. Burghardt Du Bois, "Strivings of the Negro People," *Atlantic*, August 1897, accessed December 25, 2020, https://tinyurl.com/y9epdlkz. For more on Du Bois' allusion to Wordsworth's poem, see Dolan Hubbard, ed., *The*

Souls of Black Folk: One Hundred Years Later (Columbia: University of Missouri Press, 2003), 293–94.

Chapter 7: Principle

1   Audre Lorde, *A Burst of Light, and Other Essays* (Mineola, NY: Ixia Press, 2017), 129.
2   Harrison E. Salisbury, "Fear and Hatred Grip Birmingham; Racial Tension Smoldering After Belated Sitdowns," *New York Times*, April 12, 1960, accessed December 25, 2020, https://tinyurl.com/yakcslfe; Andrew Cohen, "The Speech That Shocked Birmingham the Day After the Church Bombing," *Atlantic*, September 13, 2013, accessed December 25, 2020, https://tinyurl.com/y82skwn7.
3   Saul Alinsky, *Rules for Radicals* (New York: Vintage, 1989 [1971]), 24–25.
4   Ibid., 38.
5   Nancy Whittier, "Rethinking Coalitions: Anti-Pornography Feminists, Conservatives, and Relationships between Collaborative Adversarial Movements," *Social Problems* 61, no. 2 (May 2014): 175–93, accessed December 25, 2020, https://tinyurl.com/y78kdqyd.
6   Alinsky, *Rules for Radicals*, xix, 36. On morally prescriptive realism, see Brian Orend, *The Morality of War* (Toronto: Broadview Press, 2006), 263; Jonathan Smucker, *Hegemony How-To: A Roadmap for Radicals* (Oakland: AK Press, 2017).
7   See Elias Altman, "Joining the Chorus," *Columbia Journalism Review*, January–February 2014, accessed December 25, 2020, https://archives.cjr.org/essay/joining_the_chorus.php.
8   Malcolm X, "The Ballot or The Bullet" (speech), April 3, 1964, Cleveland, Ohio, Social Justice Speeches, accessed December 25, 2020, http://www.edchange.org/multicultural/speeches/malcolm_x_ballot.html.
9   Jeffrey Goldberg, "World Chaos and World Order: Conversations with Henry Kissinger," November 10, 2016, accessed December 25, 2020, https://tinyurl.com/ybwkfolt.
10   Dr. Martin Luther King, Jr., "Letter from a Birmingham Jail," April 16, 1963, African Studies Center—University of Pennsylvania, accessed December 25, 2020, https://www.africa.upenn.edu/Articles_Gen/Letter_Birmingham.html.
11   Jonathan Rieder, *Gospel of Freedom: Martin Luther King, Jr.'s Letter from a Birmingham Jail and the Struggle That Changed a Nation* (New York: Bloomsbury Press, 2014), 82.
12   Aleksandr I. Solzhenitsyn, *The Gulag Archipelago 1918–1956*, 3 vols., trans. Thomas P. Whitney (New York: Harper & Row, 1974).

Chapter 8: Biases

1   Paul Williams and Kenneth Ascher, "The Rainbow Connection," in *The Muppet Movie* (Los Angeles: Jim Henson Company, 1979); originally performed by Kermit the Frog (Jim Henson), accessed December 25, 2020, https://tinyurl.com/ya76oy62.
2   Review of R.J. Scott, *The Heart of Texas*, Goodreads, February 15, 2016, accessed December 25, 2020, https://www.amazon.ca/Heart-Texas-RJ-Scott/dp/1482732858.
3   See PON Staff, "Cognitive Biases in Negotiation and Conflict Resolution—Common Negotiation Mistakes," Program on Negotiation: Harvard Law School, August 10, 2020, accessed December 25, 2020, https://www.pon.harvard.edu/daily/conflict-resolution/how-ideology-leads-to-misjudging.

4   See Firewood Collective, "Sea Change: Navigating Oppression," Icarus Project, accessed December 25, 2020, https://vimeo.com/182569316.

5   "Working Families Party Director Maurice Mitchell on Defeating Trump in 2020," SURJ Chapter Network, January 10, 2020, accessed December 25, 2020, https://www.youtube.com/watch?v=vJd4XO6qOiM&feature=youtu.be.

6   "Lessons from Wakanda: What Black Panther Raises for Black Organizing," Higher Ground Change Strategies, accessed December 25, 2020, https://tinyurl.com/y9oxkjlr.

7   "Facts About Prison and People in Prison," Sentencing Project, updated August 2017, accessed December 25, 2020, https://tinyurl.com/ycva8n87.

8   Black Womxn For, Facebook, January 18, 2020, accessed December 25, 2020, https://www.facebook.com/BlackWomxnFor.

9   For context, see Charlene Carruthers, "Black Womxn For Supports Elizabeth Warren for Admitting Her Mistakes," *Teen Vogue*, February 19, 2020, accessed December 25, 2020, https://tinyurl.com/utxgydl.

Chapter 9: Rubber Meets the Road: Negotiation vs. Boycott

1   *Best Countries 2020: Global Rankings, International News and Data Insights* (Washington, DC: U.S. News and World Report, 2020), accessed December 25, 2020, https://tinyurl.com/rzo8h97.

2   The Israeli GDP includes Jews and Palestinians in Israel and the West Bank, and Jewish settlers in the West Bank, while the GDP for the West Bank does not include Jewish settlers; "GDP per Capita (Current U.S.$)—West Bank and Gaza, Israel," World Bank, accessed December 25, 2020, https://tinyurl.com/y9gkf5h6.

3   The diamonds are imported to Israel, where they are cut and exported; The Observatory of Economic Complexity, accessed December 25, 2020, https://oec.world/en/visualize/tree_map/hs92/export/show/all/7102/2017; https://oec.world/en/visualize/tree_map/hs92/export/show/all/9305/2017; https://oec.world/en/visualize/tree_map/hs92/export/show/all/8710/2017; https://oec.world/en/visualize/tree_map/hs92/export/show/all/3808/2017; https://oec.world/en/visualize/tree_map/hs92/export/show/all/0805/2017.

4   "The World Factbook: Middle East: Gaza Strip," Central Intelligence Agency, accessed February 14, 2021, https://www.cia.gov/the-world-factbook/countries/gaza-strip/#economy.

5   "The World Factbook: Middle East: Israel," Central Intelligence Agency, accessed February 14, 2021, https://www.cia.gov/the-world-factbook/countries/israel/#communications.

6   "The World Factbook: Middle East: West Bank," Central Intelligence Agency, accessed February 14, 2021, https://www.cia.gov/the-world-factbook/countries/west-bank/#communications.

7   "Economic Monitoring Report to the Ad Hoc Liaison Committee," World Bank Group, accessed February 14, 2021, https://www.un.org/unispal/wp-content/uploads/2020/06/WBADLCRPT_010620.pdf.

8   State of Israel, "Basic Law: Israel—The Nation State of The Jewish People," trans. Dr. Susan Hattis Rolef, unavailable December 25, 2020, https://knesset.gov.il/laws/special/eng/BasicLawNationState.pdf.

9   Jonathan Weisman, "American Jews and Israeli Jews Are Headed for a Messy Breakup: Is the World Ready for Another Great Schism?" *New York Times*, January 4, 2019, accessed December 25, 2020, https://tinyurl.com/yayzw79k.

10 Frank Newport, "Americans' Views of Israel Remain Tied to Religious Beliefs," Gallup, March 19, 2019, accessed December 25, 2020, https://tinyurl.com/ybyko3p4.

11 There are just under six million Jews in the US; according to Gallup, at least 5 percent, or three hundred thousand, do not support the State of Israel. Jewish Voice for Peace claims two hundred thousand supporters, see "About JVP," accessed December 25, 2020, https://jewishvoiceforpeace.org/faq. As of February 18, 2020, the largest American Jewish anti-occupation groups had the following numbers of "likes" on their Facebook pages: Jewish Voice for Peace: 573,000; Americans for Peace Now: 145,000; J Street: 45,000; If Not Now: 42,000.

12 For a brief review, see "History of Mid-East Peace Talks," BBC News, July 29, 2013, accessed December 25, 2020, https://www.bbc.com/news/world-middle-east-11103745.

13 Americans for Peace Now, "Tell Netanyahu: Trump's Vision and West Bank Annexation Threaten Israel and Peace," APN, February 6, 2020, accessed December 25, 2020, https://peacenow.org/entry.php?id=33364#.xktlxy2zou4.

14 "Economic Investment Is No Substitute for Serious Negotiations towards Real Israeli-Palestinian Peace" (press release), J Street, June 23, 2019, accessed December 25, 2020, https://tinyurl.com/yd22mew3.

15 "Palestinian Civil Society Call for BDS," BDS: Freedom, Justice, Equality, July 9, 2005, accessed December 25, 2020, https://bdsmovement.net/call.

16 "Boycott, Divestment and Sanctions," Jewish Voice for Peace, accessed December 25, 2020, https://jewishvoiceforpeace.org/boycott-divestment-and-sanctions.

17 Job 24:14.

18 Exod. 22:1.

19 Exod. 22:20.

20 bell hooks, *Teaching to Transgress: Education as the Practice of Freedom* (New York: Routledge, 1994), 61.

21 Lizzie Dearden, "Israel-Gaza Conflict: 50 Day War by Numbers," Independent, August 27, 2014, accessed December 25, 2020, https://tinyurl.com/yarqlemw.

22 Daniel Estrin, "Covertly, Israel Prepares to Fight Boycott Activists Online", AP News, February 17, 2016, https://apnews.com/article/0601a79f13e041b9b5b312ec730 63c98.

23 "The Story of King's 'Beyond Vietnam' Speech," npr, March 30, 2010, accessed February 18, 2021, https://www.npr.org/templates/story/story.php?storyId=125355148.

24 Michelle Alexander, "Time to Break the Silence on Palestine," *New York Times*, January 29, 2019, accessed December 25, 2020, https://tinyurl.com/yd4ax7vw; also see Alex Kane, "'It's Killing the Student Movement': Canary Mission's Blacklist of Pro-Palestine Activists Is Taking a Toll," Intercept, November 22, 2018, accessed December 25, 2020, https://theintercept.com/2018/11/22/israel-boycott-canary-mission-blacklist; cited in an earlier section of Alexander's op-ed.

25 "A Portrait of Jewish Americans," Pew Research Center *Religion and Public Life*, October 1, 2013, accessed December 25, 2020, https://tinyurl.com/y9kq69xz; respondents include those who identified as Jewish by religious affiliation.

Chapter 10: Conclusion

1   Audre Lorde, *The Black Unicorn: Poems* (New York: Norton, 1978), 31.

2   Thomas Jefferson et al., "Declaration of Independence" (Philadelphia, 1776), National Archives, accessed December 25, 2020, https://www.archives.gov/founding-docs/declaration-transcript.

3   "Leading with Intent: Boardsource Index of Nonprofit Board Practices," Leading with Intent, accessed December 25, 2020, https://leadingwithintent.org.

4   Jacqueline Howard, "The Disparities in How Black and White Men Die in Gun Violence, State by State," CNN, April 24, 2018, accessed December 25, 2020, https://tinyurl.com/y3a5kz63.

5   Laura Sullivan, Tatjana Meschede, Lars Dietrich, and Thomas Shapiro (Institute for Assets & Social Policy, Brandeis University), Amy Traub, Catherine Ruetschlin, and Tamara Draut (Demos), *The Racial Wealth Gap* (New York: demos.org, 2012), accessed December 25, 2020, https://tinyurl.com/ydhnxf9b; these are 2011 numbers.

6   "Linda Sarsour Writes on the Women's March and Facing Anti-Semitism," Shalom Center, November 18, 2018, accessed December 25, 2020, https://tinyurl.com/ya849gnz.

7   Pete Seeger, "Turn Turn Turn (To Everything There Is a Season)," Lyrics, accessed December 25, 2020, https://www.lyrics.com/lyric/36301467/Pete+Seeger/Turn+Turn+Turn; based on Eccles. 3:5.

8   Aly Wane, "A (Complicated) Prayer for Kobe," *America: The Jesuit Review*, January 28, 2020, accessed December 25, 2020, https://tinyurl.com/y8yz2yqx.

Index

"Passim" (literally "scattered") indicates intermittent discussion of a topic over a cluster of pages.

Acknowledgments

To Rosi Greenberg, my illustrator and collaborator, my love and appreciation for your beautiful mind, your steady hand, and your good nature.

I am so grateful to my editors. The genial, sharp, and wry political writer Mark Engler started off as my publishing advisor and mutual-accountability buddy, became my number one cheerleader, and edited the book with creativity and generosity. I am lucky to have as dear friends Daniel Laurison and Julie Greenberg who provided detailed feedback on full drafts of the book. Nina Katz fed me insights and confidence and provided attention to nuance and persistence with footnotes. My copy editor at PM Press, Michael Ryan, was keen and precise and, bonus commas notwithstanding, witty.

My comrades at Dragonfly Partners supported this project at all stages of its creation. They critiqued the model and tested the concepts in our work with progressive activists and nonprofit changemakers. Each of them reviewed a chapter. They were patient, genuine, and characteristically generous, as I clumsily split my time between writing and work over the course of two years. To Aarati Kasturirangan, Allison Budschalow, Amadee Braxton, Barbary Cook, Brianna Jones, Kris Smith, Naseem Khuri, Noah T. Winer, and Sara Joffe, my daily community in purpose and in spirit, thank you. It was Allison who had the Frederick Douglass quote on her email signature. Special thank you to Aarati for consultation on the psychology of biases and to Amadee for sharing your expertise on W. E. B. Du Bois. To Brianna, additional thanks for formatting the original bibliography, providing feedback on the book title, boosting my morale, and honoring the "beware" sign on my office door.

Other colleagues, comrades, and family members read and gave me feedback on the book proposal—Cecilie Surasky, David Headman, Dean

Johnson, and Megan Lewis—or chapters—Helena Lipstadt, Ravi de Costa, Rebecca Vilkomerson, and Susan Hackley.

It sounds corny, but I do thank you all for the discernment and wisdom you brought and ask readers to blame me for the places I didn't take my editors' and readers' good advice.

Over the course of a decade and a half, the students in my Peace and Conflict classes at West Chester University asked and answered the questions in this book a hundred times a semester. The model emerged from these discussions. Thank you to my former students Kevin Mann, Ben Kraut, and Glenn Chon for research support. Thank you to Joan Woolfrey for wisdom on ethics and for trusting me.

Among my teachers have been Arthur Waskow, Barry Oshry, Brian Mandell, Celeste Schenck, Dennis Dalton, George Lakey, Heather Hurlburt, Khaled Salim, Marshall Ganz, and Tim Hayes. Though their names are absent from the book, they helped develop my understanding of conflict and political change. It was at the Kennedy School in 2004, sitting in Marshall's community organizing class and thinking about my homework for Brian's negotiation class, that I first asked myself: Why can't I form a coherent sentence that reflects the wisdom of these two worlds, protest and negotiation, both of which feel to me like home? That question was the seed from which this book blossomed.

For helpful conversations on the talking-fighting model, thank you to Aly Wane on fighting with compassion, Andrew Rehfeld on Walzer's contribution to Weber's problem of dirty hands, Erica Dobbs on talking-fighting tension in the real world, Brian McHugh on labor controlling demand, Gretjen Clausing on the Comcast campaign, James Schamus for cocktail party philosophy, JD Davids on AIDS activism, Megan Lewis on the dilemmas of white leadership, Sarah Halley on rank, and Zoe Greenberg on what to call the columns.

My two splendid children Nava EtShalom and Yonah EtShalom gave me feedback on stories and theory. Our spiral cycles of give and take have influenced my thinking and this book even more.

In particular, to the poet and critic Nava EtShalom for the John Samuelson union video and a million other pieces of advice, and for allocating spoons to editing my preface at the midnight hour, my deep respect and gratitude.

Doug Stone and Esteban Kelly, thank you for taking a risk and endorsing the book with your forewords and a bigger risk betting on the opposition.

Thank you to Steven Stothard at PM Press for being charming and eager at the outset and lovely to work with, and to Esteban Kelly for steering me in PM's direction. Thanks also to PM's Brian Layng and Stephanie Pasvankias, and to John Yates and Rosi Greenberg for patience and creativity in designing the cover. Thanks to Andrew Boyd, Rep. Chris Rabb, Chuck Collins, Jenny Beer, Matthew Lyons, and Stellan Vinthagen for advice along the publishing road.

For permission to tell your stories, thanks to Aly Wane, Jethro Heiko, Malek, and Raed Jarrar. Thanks to Kati Sipp, Makani Themba, and Malkia Devich Cyril for permission to print your wise words. Thanks to Buster Benson for your beautiful chart of biases, and props to Fabricio Rodriguez, the quintessential organizer, for inspiration.

My JVP comrades have been my strategy muses over the past fifteen years. Special thanks to Cecilie Surasky and Noah T. Winer for encouraging my thinking about theories of change.

Shout-out to my SURJ Pod for inspiration and confidence on learning to live and theorize responsibly as a white person. Shout-out too to my colleagues past and present at CMPartners under whose wing I learned to teach the skill of negotiation: Elizabeth McClintock, Eric Henry, Jim Tull, Ken Hyatt, and Tom Schaub. Gratitude to my teachers' teacher, the late Roger Fisher.

Thank you to the kind people who, wittingly or not, hosted my writing time: Kathy and Andy at Lake Owassa, Barbary for the cabin in Krumville, the librarians at the United Lutheran Seminary and Chestnut Hill College libraries, and the day traders in second floor politics at the Parkway Central Library.

Gratitude to the generations ahead of me: my beloved father E. David Subar died at age ninety-five during my writing of this book. We spoke infrequently and didn't share an analysis of the world, but we shared deep curiosity about how differently people saw things, and he would always ask how the book was going. After he finally retired from his engineering career and moved from Rochester to Jerusalem at age eighty-three, he continued to wear his Miller Lighting notepad in his shirt pocket to record names and nouns and news he didn't want to forget. Despite our political differences, he would ask me to repeat the details of my work with Palestinian activists and negotiators to be sure he got his notes right.

My mother's sister, Aunt Mina, has been a life-long booster and backer of my kids and my parenting life. When, at twenty-five, I needed a landing place with two young children, she set up her big Brooklyn basement for us with trademark dry wit and wraparound home front support. I am grateful to include Fionnuala Cook here as foundational to my support system. She is as empathetic a mother-in-law and friend as a person could hope to have.

It's weird how consistently people thank their main squeeze at this point, if they have one. I am so used to not hewing to convention that I wish I could do this differently. But, as it just so happens, I want to thank my life partner Barbary Cook, above all. She of the brutally fierce life force and equally brutal sense of humor inside a web of grave illnesses and the biggest heart in the universe. She protected me from some of my guilt and all of my responsibilities while I wrote this book. To Barbary.

About the Contributors

Rebecca Subar taught Peace and Conflict Studies at West Chester University from 2005 to 2019. She is a senior partner at Dragonfly, where a multiracial band of consultants supports organizations that make social change. She has coached leaders of political advocacy groups, large and small, on their race consciousness, their organization's growth, and their strategy for changing the world.

Rosi Greenberg is a graphic facilitator and leadership trainer. She holds a master's in public policy from the Harvard Kennedy School and works with C-suite executives, community organizers, nonprofits, philanthropists, youth groups, and political campaigns, helping them to connect deeply and make creative, systemic change.

Esteban Kelly is the executive director for the US Federation of Worker Cooperatives and a founding member in AORTA, a worker-owned co-op whose facilitation supports organizations fighting for social justice and a solidarity economy. He received a Social Innovation Award for Public Policy and is an advisor to the Movement for Black Lives policy table.

Douglas Stone has taught negotiation and conflict management at Harvard Law School since 1993. He is a coauthor of two *New York Times* bestsellers, *Difficult Conversations: How to Discuss What Matters Most* (Penguin Books, 2000) and *Thanks for the Feedback: The Science and Art of Receiving Feedback Well* (Viking, 2014), both with Bruce Patton and Sheila Heen, and consults around the world on topics of communication, mediation, and leadership.

About Dragonfly Partners

Dragonfly Partners helps changemakers—both inside and outside the political system—to get "unstuck" and work through strategic, organizational, and interpersonal challenges. We offer advice and support on organizational change, conflict, and strategy; we coach leaders, lead strategic planning processes, and mediate disputes. We support organizations, helping them to choose thoughtful and brave ways to match their realities to their values and to rise to face racial inequity in their programmatic work and in their internal structures and practices.

Our clients are advocacy groups, foundations, universities, faith-based organizations, labor unions, coalitions, and government agencies. Our multiracial team brings experience from the fields of community organizing, policy advocacy, anti-oppression coaching and training, organizational development, social work, resource generation, and conflict management.

To work with us, write to info@Dragonfly-Partners.com.

ABOUT PM PRESS

PM Press is an independent, radical publisher of books and media to educate, entertain, and inspire. Founded in 2007 by a small group of people with decades of publishing, media, and organizing experience, PM Press amplifies the voices of radical authors, artists, and activists. Our aim is to deliver bold political ideas and vital stories to all walks of life and arm the dreamers to demand the impossible. We have sold millions of copies of our books, most often one at a time, face to face. We're old enough to know what we're doing and young enough to know what's at stake. Join us to create a better world.

PM Press
PO Box 23912
Oakland, CA 94623
www.pmpress.org

PM Press in Europe
europe@pmpress.org
www.pmpress.org.uk

FRIENDS OF PM PRESS

These are indisputably momentous times—the financial
system is melting down globally and the Empire is
stumbling. Now more than ever there is a vital need for
radical ideas.

In the years since its founding—and on a mere shoestring—
PM Press has risen to the formidable challenge of publishing and distributing
knowledge and entertainment for the struggles ahead. With over 450 releases
to date, we have published an impressive and stimulating array of literature, art,
music, politics, and culture. Using every available medium, we've succeeded in
connecting those hungry for ideas and information to those putting them into
practice.

Friends of PM allows you to directly help impact, amplify, and revitalize the
discourse and actions of radical writers, filmmakers, and artists. It provides us
with a stable foundation from which we can build upon our early successes and
provides a much-needed subsidy for the materials that can't necessarily pay
their own way. You can help make that happen—and receive every new title
automatically delivered to your door once a month—by joining as a Friend of PM
Press. And, we'll throw in a free T-shirt when you sign up.

Here are your options:

- **$30 a month** Get all books and pamphlets plus 50% discount on all webstore
  purchases

- **$40 a month** Get all PM Press releases (including CDs and DVDs) plus 50%
  discount on all webstore purchases

- **$100 a month** Superstar—Everything plus PM merchandise, free downloads, and
  50% discount on all webstore purchases

For those who can't afford $30 or more a month, we have **Sustainer Rates** at $15,
$10, and $5. Sustainers get a free PM Press T-shirt and a 50% discount on all
purchases from our website.

Your Visa or Mastercard will be billed once a month, until you tell us to stop.
Or until our efforts succeed in bringing the revolution around. Or the financial
meltdown of Capital makes plastic redundant. Whichever comes first.

Re:Imagining Change: How to Use Story-Based Strategy to Win Campaigns, Build Movements, and Change the World

Patrick Reinsborough & Doyle Canning

ISBN: 978-1-62963-384-8
$18.95   224 pages

Re:Imagining Change provides resources, theory, hands-on tools, and illuminating case studies for the next generation of innovative change-makers. This unique book explores how culture, media, memes, and narrative intertwine with social change strategies, and offers practical methods to amplify progressive causes in the popular culture.

Re:Imagining Change is an inspirational inside look at the trailblazing methodology developed by the Center for Story-based Strategy over fifteen years of their movement building partnerships. This practitioner's guide is an impassioned call to innovate our strategies for confronting the escalating social and ecological crises of the twenty-first century. This new, expanded second edition includes updated examples from the frontlines of social movements and provides the reader with easy-to-use tools to change the stories they care about most.

"All around us the old stories are failing, crumbling in the face of lived experience and scientific reality. But what stories will replace them? That is the subject of this crucial book: helping readers to tell irresistible stories about deep change—why it is needed and what it will look like. The Story-based Strategy team has been doing this critical work for fifteen years, training an entire generation in transformative communication. This updated edition of Re:Imagining Change *is a thrilling addition to the activist tool kit."*
—Naomi Klein, author of *This Changes Everything: Capitalism vs. the Climate*

"This powerful and useful book is an invitation to harness the transformative power of stories by examining social change strategy through the lens of narrative. Re:Imagining Change *is an essential resource to make efforts for fundamental social change more enticing, compelling, and effective. It's a potent how-to book for anyone working to create a better world."*
—Ilyse Hogue, president, NARAL Pro-Choice America

"Brilliant and invaluable. George Lakoff introduced the progressive movement to the power of framing. Doyle Canning and Patrick Reinsborough take framing to a far more powerful level and provide practical tools essential to the success of every progressive organization that seeks to bring forth a world of peace and justice. It gets my highest recommendation."
—David Korten, author of *The Great Turning: From Empire to Earth Community*

Facilitating Group Learning: Strategies for Success with Diverse Learners, Second Edition

George Lakey with a Foreword by Mark Leier

ISBN: 978-1-62963-826-3
$20.00   320 pages

From the acclaimed coauthor of *A Manual for Direct Action* comes *Facilitating Group Learning*, an essential resource designed to help educators, trainers, workshop leaders, and anyone who assists groups to learn. George Lakey presents the core principles and proven techniques of direct education, an approach he developed for effectively teaching adults in groups. To illustrate how it works in action, Lakey includes a wealth of compelling stories from his vast experience facilitating groups in a variety of situations.

Direct education cuts through the pretense and needless complications that can distance learners from subject matter. It removes false expectations (for example, that kinesthetic learners will strongly benefit from slide presentations) and false assumptions (for example, that a group is simply the sum of the individuals). This approach focuses the encounter between teacher and group; it replaces scattered attention—of a teacher preoccupied with curriculum and participants preoccupied with distractions—with gathered attention.

Unlike in other books on group facilitation, the author emphasizes critical issues related to diversity, as well as authenticity and emotions. Step by step, this groundbreaking book describes how to design effective learning experiences and shows what it takes to facilitate them. Ultimately, it brings all the elements of the author's direct education approach together.

Facilitating Group Learning also contains material on sustaining the educator, addresses working with social movements, and includes the Training for Change toolkit of group learning techniques.

"If you want to be a soldier, you can go to West Point. If you want to be a nonviolent change-maker—well, this is an awfully good place to start. George Lakey has been near the center of American resistance for decades, and so he has both remarkable stories and remarkable insights—not to mention some remarkable colleagues who add their perspective to this necessary manual!"
—Bill McKibben, cofounder of 350.org

We Have Not Been Moved: Resisting Racism and Militarism in 21st Century America

Edited by Elizabeth 'Betita' Martínez,
Mandy Carter & Matt Meyer with
an Introduction by Cornel West and
Afterwords/poems by Alice Walker &
Sonia Sanchez

ISBN: 978-1-60486-480-9
$29.95   608 pages

We Have Not Been Moved is a compendium addressing the two leading pillars of U.S. Empire. Inspired by the work of Dr. Martin Luther King Jr., who called for a "true revolution of values" against the racism, militarism, and materialism which he saw as the heart of a society "approaching spiritual death," this book recognizes that—for the most part—the traditional peace movement has not been moved far beyond the half-century-old call for a deepening critique of its own prejudices. While reviewing the major points of intersection between white supremacy and the war machine through both historic and contemporary articles from a diverse range of scholars and activists, the editors emphasize what needs to be done now to move forward for lasting social change. Produced in collaboration with the War Resisters League, the book also examines the strategic possibilities of radical transformation through revolutionary nonviolence.

Among the historic texts included are rarely-seen writings by antiracist icons such as Anne Braden, Barbara Deming, and Audre Lorde, as well as a dialogue between Dr. King, revolutionary nationalist Robert F. Williams, Dave Dellinger, and Dorothy Day. Never-before-published pieces appear from civil rights and gay rights organizer Bayard Rustin and from celebrated U.S. pacifist supporter of Puerto Rican sovereignty Ruth Reynolds. Additional articles making their debut in this collection include new essays by and interviews with Fred Ho, Jose Lopez, Joel Kovel, Francesca Fiorentini and Clare Bayard, David McReynolds, Greg Payton, Gwendolyn Zoharah Simmons, Ellen Barfield, Jon Cohen, Suzanne Ross, Sachio Ko-Yin, Edward Hasbrouck, Dean Johnson, and Dan Berger. Other contributions include work by Andrea Dworkin, Mumia Abu-Jamal, Starhawk, Andrea Smith, John Stoltenberg, Vincent Harding, Liz McAlister, Victor Lewis, Matthew Lyons, Tim Wise, Dorothy Cotton, Ruth Wilson Gilmore, Kenyon Farrow, Frida Berrigan, David Gilbert, Chris Crass, and many others. Peppered throughout the anthology are original and new poems by Chrystos, Dylcia Pagan, Malkia M'Buzi Moore, Sarah Husein, Mary Jane Sullivan, Liz Roberts, and the late Marilyn Buck.

White Lives Matter Most: And Other "Little" White Lies

Matt Meyer with a Foreword by Sonia Sanchez

ISBN: 978-1-62963-540-8
$14.95   128 pages

Modern-day movements to end racism in the U.S. seem sadly doomed to fail. If more fundamental approaches to social change and more sober analysis of U.S. history are not considered, our efforts will lead to continued fragmentation—or worse. The essays in this book—written by lifelong anti-imperialist organizer, educator, and author Matt Meyer—reveal the successful strategies and methods of multigenerational and multitendency coalitions used in recent campaigns to free Puerto Rican and Black Panther political prisoners, confront neo-Nazis in Charlottesville, and many more.

Meyer's reflections on the need for a new, intensified solidarity consciousness and accountability among white folks provide a provocative and urgent challenge. These essays—some coauthored by Black Lives Matter and Ferguson Truth Telling leaders Natalie Jeffers and David Ragland, Puerto Rican professor Ana López, Muslim interfaith activist Sahar Alsahlani, and Afro-Asian cultural icon Fred Ho—offer up-to-the-minute insights. Read on, and get ready for hope in the context of hard work.

"This legendary freedom fighter brings together the best of the peace movement and the best of the anti-racist movement."
—Cornel West

"The stories Matt Meyer tells should be listened to by all people who work for freedom and justice: not just for the few, but for everybody."
—Talib Kweli, hip hop artist, entrepreneur, and social activist

"The rich and still evolving tradition of revolutionary pacifism, effectively sampled in these thoughtful and penetrating essays, offers the best hope we have for overcoming threats that are imminent and grim, and for moving on to create a society that is more just and free. These outstanding contributions should be carefully pondered, and taken to heart as a call for action."
—Noam Chomsky, on We Have Not Been Moved

"This book demonstrates the scope of the Panthers' intellectual gifts as well as the compassion and revolutionary spirit at the center of their radical grassroots activism."
—Publishers Weekly on Look for Me in the Whirlwind

Towards Collective Liberation: Anti-Racist Organizing, Feminist Praxis, and Movement Building Strategy

Chris Crass
with an Introduction by Chris Dixon and
Foreword by Roxanne Dunbar-Ortiz

ISBN: 978-1-60486-654-4
$20.00   320 pages

Towards Collective Liberation: Anti-Racist Organizing, Feminist Praxis, and Movement Building Strategy is for activists engaging with dynamic questions of how to create and support effective movements for visionary systemic change. Chris Crass's collection of essays and interviews presents us with powerful lessons for transformative organizing through offering a firsthand look at the challenges and the opportunities of anti-racist work in white communities, feminist work with men, and bringing women of color feminism into the heart of social movements. Drawing on two decades of personal activist experience and case studies of anti-racist social justice organizations, Crass insightfully explores ways of transforming divisions of race, class, and gender into catalysts for powerful vision, strategy, and movement building in the United States today.

"In his writing and organizing, Chris Crass has been at the forefront of building the grassroots, multi-racial, feminist movements for justice we need. Towards Collective Liberation *takes on questions of leadership, building democratic organizations, and movement strategy, on a very personal level that invites us all to experiment and practice the way we live our values while struggling for systemic change."*
—Elizabeth 'Betita' Martinez, founder of the Institute for Multiracial Justice and author of *De Colores Means All of Us: Latina Views for a Multi-Colored Century*

"Chris Crass goes into the grassroots to produce a political vision that will catalyze political change. These are words from the heart, overflowing onto the streets."
—Vijay Prashad, author of *Darker Nations: A People's History of the Third World*

"A deeply important, engaged, and learned defense of anarchism, class politics, and anti-racism. Grounded in study, organizing, and struggle, Towards Collective Liberation *is a significant contribution to the recent history of the U.S. left."*
—David Roediger, author of *Wages of Whiteness*

"In his activism and writing, Chris Crass has been able to articulate and practice a transformative model for social change. Guided by a vision of collective liberation that centers the experience and leadership of women of color, Chris has done groundbreaking work to realize the revolutionary potential of grassroots multiracial alliances."
—Harsha Walia, co-founder of No One Is Illegal and Radical Desis

Teaching Resistance: Radicals, Revolutionaries, and Cultural Subversives in the Classroom

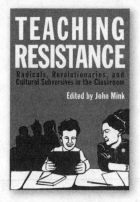

Edited by John Mink

ISBN: 978-1-62963-709-9
$24.95   416 pages

Teaching Resistance is a collection of the voices of activist educators from around the world who engage inside and outside the classroom from pre-kindergarten to university and emphasize teaching radical practice from the field. Written in accessible language, this book is for anyone who wants to explore new ways to subvert educational systems and institutions, collectively transform educational spaces, and empower students and other teachers to fight for genuine change. Topics include community self-defense, Black Lives Matter and critical race theory, intersections between punk/DIY subculture and teaching, ESL, anarchist education, Palestinian resistance, trauma, working-class education, prison teaching, the resurgence of (and resistance to) the Far Right, special education, antifascist pedagogies, and more.

Edited by social studies teacher, author, and punk musician John Mink, the book features expanded entries from the monthly column in the politically insurgent punk magazine *Maximum Rocknroll*, plus new works and extensive interviews with subversive educators. Contributing teachers include Michelle Cruz Gonzales, Dwayne Dixon, Martín Sorrondeguy, Alice Bag, Miriam Klein Stahl, Ron Scapp, Kadijah Means, Mimi Nguyen, Murad Tamini, Yvette Felarca, Jessica Mills, and others, all of whom are unified against oppression and readily use their classrooms to fight for human liberation, social justice, systemic change, and true equality.

Royalties will be donated to Teachers 4 Social Justice: t4sj.org

"Teaching Resistance *brings us the voices of activist educators who are fighting back inside and outside of the classroom. The punk rock spirit of this collection of concise, hard-hitting essays is bound to stir up trouble.*"
—Mark Bray, historian, author of *Antifa: The Anti-Fascist Handbook* and coeditor of *Anarchist Education and the Modern School: A Francisco Ferrer Reader*

"*Where was* Teaching Resistance *when I was in school? This essay collection both makes a compelling case for why radical classrooms are necessary and lays out how they can be put into practice. A perfect guide for educators and anyone working with young people, this book vitally also speaks to the student's experience. Even for the kid-adverse activists among us,* Teaching Resistance *reminds us that kids can be our comrades if we meet them halfway. The younger generations deserve more from us— this is the primer for how to start providing it.*"
—Shawna Potter, singer for War on Women, author of *Making Spaces Safer*

Raising Free People: Unschooling as Liberation and Healing Work

Akilah S. Richards
with a Foreword by Bayo Akomolafe

ISBN: 978-1-62963-833-1
$17.00   192 pages

No one is immune to the byproducts of compulsory schooling and standardized testing. And while reform may be a worthy cause for some, it is not enough for countless others still trying to navigate the tyranny of what schooling has always been. *Raising Free People* argues that we need to build and work within systems truly designed for any human to learn, grow, socialize, and thrive, regardless of age, ability, background, or access to money.

Families and conscious organizations across the world are healing generations of school wounds by pivoting into self-directed, intentional community-building, and *Raising Free People* shows you exactly how unschooling can help facilitate this process.

Individual experiences influence our approach to parenting and education, so we need more than the rules, tools, and "bad adult" guilt trips found in so many parenting and education books. We need to reach behind our behaviors to seek and find our triggers; to examine and interrupt the ways that social issues such as colonization still wreak havoc on our ability to trust ourselves, let alone children. *Raising Free People* explores examples of the transition from school or homeschooling to unschooling, how single parents and people facing financial challenges unschool successfully, and the ways unschooling allows us to address generational trauma and unlearn the habits we mindlessly pass on to children.

In these detailed and unabashed stories and insights, Richards examines the ways that her relationships to blackness, decolonization, and healing work all combine to form relationships and enable community-healing strategies rooted in an unschooling practice. This is how millions of families center human connection, practice clear and honest communication, and raise children who do not grow up to feel that they narrowly survived their childhoods.

"This is an insightful, brilliant book by one of today's most inspiring leaders in the realm of Self-Directed Education. We see here how respecting children, listening to them, and learning from them can revolutionize our manner of parenting and remove the blinders imposed by the forced schooling that we nearly all experienced. I recommend it to everyone who cares about children, freedom, and the future of humanity."
—Peter Gray, research professor of psychology at Boston College, author of *Free to Learn*